Dr. Rosalind Osgad
5/21/2022

Dr. Rosalind Osred
5/9/1949

Story Behind the Story

How a multigenerational, multicultural, multidenominational approach can reach women

Dr. Rosalind Osgood

Library of Congress Control Number: 2011909686

I dedicate this book to my late grandmother, Agnes Wade, who passed away on May 2, 2007. You are no longer here in body, but I keep your spirit close. You were a woman of prayer and love, a great woman of God. You invested in the lives of so many people. You willingly made a plethora of sacrifices so I could have life better than you did. I miss you dearly.

•

I also dedicate this book to the women of my family: my biological mother, Linda Wilson; my aunt, Reita Shannon; my sister Shennette Huff; my children's grandmother, Bonnie Sheffield; and my cousin, Babette Davis. You all have taught me many valuable life lessons.

Contents

Acknowledgments

No one progresses through life alone. When one is matriculating through life, where do you start to thank those who joined you, walked before you, and helped you along the way?

Over the years, I have had many individuals to encourage me to write a book to record the miseries and miracles of my life. With the help of God and numerous men and women I have been able to overcome obstacles, optimize opportunities, and obtain outstanding outcomes. So at last here it is.

This book and its pages are "thanks" to the thousands of you who have helped make my life what it is today. Much of what I have learned over the years came as a result of being a mother to three outstanding and awesome children: Shennette, Anthony, and Gabriel Sheffield, who are the wind beneath my wings. I thank Mr. Ronald Johnson who has brought much joy to my life over the past two years.

Additionally, I thank one of the most brilliant minds and prophetic voices of today, my father in the ministry, the legendary Dr. Mack King Carter. He taught me to pursue knowledge, to prepare and preach the Gospel with clarity, and to be unwavering in my service to humanity. I also thank the amazing men and women who wake up with me each morning on the Women Reaching Women Word Network. It is through their preaching, teaching, prayers, and support that I continue to gain and grow.

It's strange to think that I have been working nonstop for the past 22 years and that this is my first book. The catalyst that made me complete this work was my pastor who challenged me to get it done. Thanks, Pastor Marcus D. Davidson. And then comes Monica Tagore, my editor with an abundance of talents and patience. She read my drafts, understood my message, and kept me working on the book.

I have poured my heart and soul into these pages. I am indescribably grateful to God for His favor in my life. So now I pray that my words touch your heart, soul, and mind.

Foreword

The essence of any literary work is when it is concretized in the life of the writer. This has been achieved in this work by my daughter in the faith, the Reverend Dr. Rosalind Osgood. As her former pastor, I can personally chronicle her sojourn from the streets to spiritual maturity. She is duly qualified academically, theologically, and experientially to speak on the plight of women.

Though all women can glean nuggets for their enhancement from reading this book, its main focus is women of the oppressed community. While feminist theology deals with the vicissitudes of the majority community, this book espouses a womanist theological perspective which deals with the oppression and the depression of women of ebony hue.

This book is more than a regurgitation of pain. It is a clarion call for women to become educated and dedicated to the proposition that women must be free. If we are all going to be free, then women must be extricated from all semblances of oppression.

Liberation theology simply means salvation at the vertical and the horizontal levels.

While some liberation theologies have a Marxian praxis, this work is unashamedly Christocentric. Some radical feminists embrace an atheistic or an agnostic perspective. However, this author believes that the greatest hope for African American women is Jesus of Nazareth.

The author gives us a practical and a poignant analysis of existential reality. It is a mirror that gives a fresh word that is salvific to all who will believe. The pain and the potential are like twins, waiting to be delivered from the womb of a pregnant woman.

There is no room for bitterness, but a summons to become better.

Both men and women are incentivized to become agents of change. Neither men nor women can authentically become comrades in liberation until we free each other. This book then is a gauntlet and a guide that leads to the personhood of women. Beyond this, it is a manifesto for change.

Therefore, those who read this work will be blessed, and those who will enact its principles will become better. And those who are consistently pragmatic will be transformed.

Dr. Mack King Carter
Pastor Emeritus
New Mount Olive Baptist Church
Fort Lauderdale, Florida

Introduction

She sits in a front pew dressed beautifully, looking like the picture of health and happiness. Except she is not. Inside, emotional turmoil has her depressed, devastated, and desperate as she silently prays for a miracle.

Another sister tiptoes into church after service has begun and looks for a spot toward the back. She wasn't sure if she'd come, but somehow she made it. She feels invisible as she sits down and hungrily searches the crowd for a face that smiles back at her.

Yet another sister stands before the congregation, singing an old hymn of the church, "Amazing Grace," in a way that brings tears to everyone's eyes, including her own. All those in attendance marvel at the way she can belt out those lyrics, never realizing the feeling she puts into her songs is because she knows the true meaning of the words: She has been beaten. She has been battered. She has been bruised. But she is a beneficiary of God's amazing grace. She once was lost but now she's found; 'twas blind but now she sees.

Women have to matriculate through many phases of life. Familial, professional, and hormonal changes place women in the grips of the practical pains of life. I define practical pain as pain that impacts us mentally, spiritually, and physically. It oftentimes makes us depressed and discombobulated. This type of pain is so overwhelming that we seek relief through food, drugs, sex, shopping, etc. On any given day when I go to preach at a church, whether it is my own or one where I am a guest, I know before I stand up that I will see a woman who is hurting. The reality is that women are hurting in every congregation. Women are literally fighting for their lives.

Sometimes the pain is the hurt of failing health. A woman can walk into a doctor's office feeling that life is going pretty well, only to walk out with devastating news and what feels very much like a death sentence. Another woman may be dealing with emotional or mental hurt as she tries to process the termination of her most recent relationship and navigate through the feelings of letting go while wanting to hold on. Yet another woman, like the singer in the example above, may be dealing with the weight of broken promises, physical hurts, and cruel heartache, all wrapped into one.

Whether it's physical, emotional, mental, or spiritual, the pain is real. And it is literally killing women in churches worldwide.

That is the reason for this book. I have a passion to reach as many women as I can. I want to take the gospel from the pulpit to the pavement and touch lives in a unique way. Women reaching women is the theme of my work as I strive to let women know God loves them. We are at a critical point in history. We cannot allow our pain to make us miss this moment. We are writing the days of our lives. Some of us are young and restless. Others of us are bold and beautiful or just living day by day as the world turns. So we must be intentional in our actions to reach other women. I believe God has called us women to influence history. We can shape thinking in a way that launches another woman into her destiny. Throughout history, women have always been on the scene, but in far too many instances, we have not been given respect or credibility. We've been seen as second-class, second-rate, and second thoughts.

If we just use the resources amongst ourselves, we can change that. We don't have to play second to anyone. We can uplift, encourage, and empower each other to live the lives God has created us to live. Sisters — Black, White, Hispanic, Asian, Native American — all need to know there is a solution for their pain. God is still a balm in Gilead. He can heal us everywhere we hurt.

Women are in the majority in most of our churches, yet the needs of women are not being met. Women take care of everyone else around us, but when it comes to someone taking care of us, we are left wanting. This book is a call to action to women worldwide that we begin to seriously bond with each other — iron sharpening iron. So come on, sisters. Let's unite and help each other overcome past hurt, present pain, and perpetual losses. Join me in this multigenerational, multicultural, multidenominational mega movement to support, strengthen, and serve women all over the world.

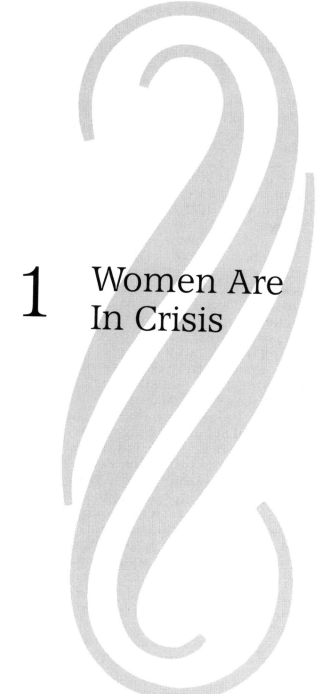

1 Women Are In Crisis

When I see statistics that show millions of children being raised by female heads of household are dropping out of school at an accelerated rate in certain parts of the country, I know something must be done. When I see reports that girls who used to get pregnant at 16 are now getting pregnant at 9 from men 30 and 40 years old, I am frantic to find a solution. According to the American Cancer Society more than 1 in 3 women will be stricken with cancer in their lifetime. According to the Center for Disease Control, more than 278,000 women and adolescent girls in this country are living with HIV; and almost 94,000 American women and girls with AIDS have died since the epidemic began. Women and girls of color — especially Black women and girls—bear a disproportionately heavy burden of HIV/ AIDS. According to the National Center on Minority Health and Health Disparities March 2010 seminar series, 1 in 4 women will die of heart disease. Over 1 million women are now under some type of criminal supervision. Forty percent of women currently in jail reported being physically or sexually abused prior to age 18. Of all individuals who report rape and sexual assault, 78 percent are women. Women are at the center of each of these facts. I see these statistics and I have a burden — or holy contentment, as Pastor Marcus Davidson would say —to change them. But I know they will not change without women being intentional about reaching out to other women. We must come together. We must use our diversities to create unity. We must use our gifts rather than our deficiencies to rebuild our families and neighborhoods. We must become creatures of associational life. According to John McKnight, associational life is groups of people voluntarily coming together to do some good. We are the remnant of social capital that God created to be the fabric of ministry, mission, and marriage. Thus, our current existential realities of poverty, injustice, lack of family values and illiteracy will only improve if we improve. It is a direct relationship. As we get better, our children, spouses, neighborhoods, and churches get better.

Women are in crisis.

Women in many instances are raising most of our children in single parent home environments. In many cases, women are doing the best they can. But the results still aren't good. More than half of those children will not graduate high school. Many teenage girls are getting pregnant and having babies before they truly understand what a menstrual cycle is, suggesting that they themselves are mothers in need of something more. So our communities are plagued with uneducated children, babies having babies, and devastating diseases.

What this means is that if what we are doing is not working, we've got to do something different. We have to shift from being reactors to being revolutionizers. Things must change. Our children's future demands that we change. We must be intentional with our choices. It's not enough to wander through life and let things happen to us. Because if we simply continue to react to what goes on, then we will always be on the losing end of an equation. And so will our children.

I don't speak in the abstract here.

I speak from real-life experience.

When I look at my own life 21 years ago, I see that God placed women on my path who could guide, inspire, and empower me to live a better life. I was in a really bad place at that time: I was homeless, addicted to drugs, and running in and out of jail.

I have been in a state of incomprehensible demoralization. I have walked this walk of desperation and hopelessness. I have felt the emotions of failure, defeat, and sadness. That's why I can write this book. I can speak to any woman's heart and let her know that the low place she is in now does not have to be the place she ends up. She can move to a better place. I know because it happened for me. I echo the words of the psalmist, "weeping may endure for a night but joy cometh in the morning."

I was a student at Florida A&M University, but I dropped out in my last year, pregnant. I got married to cover up the pregnancy. I was in the grips of drug addiction. I was making one bad decision after another. I ultimately ended up homeless, living in boarded-up buildings, battling drugs and alcohol. I was even selling drugs — so not only was I using them, but I was distributing them to others.

I was arrested several times. I was going in and out of

jail for drug possession. Clearly, my life was a mess. I had gone from this young woman with so much promise — my grandparents had poured all of their love, time, and money into me — to a repeat offender.

My body eventually showed the effects of my unhealthy lifestyle, as I weighed maybe 65 pounds soaking wet. My lipstick weighed more than I did. I was a sack of skin loosely holding together some bones. My skin was lifeless and my eyes hollow. When I refused to give up the drugs, I found myself on the Fort Lauderdale Beach robbing people at gunpoint. My life was so chaotic. I lived to use and used to live. I would drop off my children at relatives' and not return for weeks.

I finally hit bottom when drugs no longer allowed me to alter my mood. Getting high lost its effect. At last, I was desperate enough to change. At this time I had violated probation and missed court for a new charge. I went to my grandmother and she made provisions to get me to Volusia County to turn myself in, as I had an outstanding warrant for my arrest. We arrived at 5 minutes to 5. The judge said, "The only place I have for you is jail."

"OK," I said. I was desperate to stop feeling what I was feeling. So I went to jail and did what felt comfortable: I immediately got into a confrontation. It was normal. I would often start fights within the first hour of being in the unit.

The argument was with my cellmate, who told me I looked like a monster. I wanted the top bunk, where she was. Whether it was the words she uttered or the fact that I wanted the bed she was sleeping in, something ignited anger within me. We got into a fight and the jailhouse personnel separated us. When she left, I plopped down on the bottom bunk and looked around for something to get into. I rummaged through the few possessions she left behind and ended up with her Bible.

I flipped to the gospel according to Matthew and started trying to read the model prayer. But I couldn't read it. This was after three years of college. I could not make out the words. I slowly walked over to the mirror on the wall and the dark, sunken eyes staring back at me said, "We are going to die."

I had become the bum on the street. I was eating out of

Dumpsters, living in cardboard boxes or treetops. And now, I was locked up.

I went back to my bottom bunk and sat down. My grandmother had always taught me that when I get to a place in life where all else fails, I could trust Jesus. So I decided to try Him.

"Lord, I don't know if you are real or not but I need help. I can't go on like this."

I curled up on the bed and fell asleep. I woke up the next morning and grabbed my cellmate's Bible again. This time, I could read the prayer a little better. That said to me that God had heard my cry. He was allowing me to have reading comprehension.

The second day, someone from the jail came and said they were releasing me to go to a rehab center in Broward County called Broward Alcohol Rehabilitation Center (BARC). That was another sign that God heard me. He was opening doors for me, where just 24 hours ago, nothing seemed to be available.

I had been in rehab several times already, but there was a difference this time. Before, I hadn't been serious. I had just been hiding out from the police or drug dealers. This time, I was ready to listen to what they told me to do. One of my counselors, a gentleman named Guy Wheeler, got in my face. "You stop cursing out folks!" he said. Maybe my quick temper and fiery tongue need to be put in check, I thought to myself. I said, "OK."

When I got out of rehab, I went to the twelve step meetings. I listened. I related. Everything my counselors told me to do, I did.

By this time, I was pregnant again. I already had two children, a daughter and a son. They lived with my first husband. My first marriage was a vicious cycle. I would leave, get sober, go back, get pregnant, relapse, and leave again. Now I was again living with my maternal grandmother and grandfather, two people who loved me unconditionally. Each time I would go to jail, my grandmother would slap me upside the head, but she would be there for me. She was an outstanding mother. Because of her I would often think about my children. I knew I needed to change to be there for my children. I had phone contact with them when I was in rehab and my first husband sometimes brought them to see me.

But I needed to be with them on a regular basis. When my daughter fell sick and wanted no one but her mother, my first husband brought her to me. From then on, I was with my children. I knew nobody could raise them the way I could, so I was finally ready to be a fulltime mother. I did not relapse again. I am totally convinced that God gave me my children to save my life. To this day, they are still the wind beneath my wings.

About two years into recovery, I attended a seminar where they talked about the disease aspect of addiction. Addicts have allergic reactions to certain chemicals and our bodies begin to crave those substances. In my case, drugs and alcohol. I had an epiphany: I realized that if I don't do the first one, I don't have to worry about the second or third. I had no interest in picking up those old habits again.

I was working part-time at McDonald's, pregnant, and going to 12-step recovery meetings. I had my third child in May 1990, and he was born clean. As a reward for staying clean, the judge granted me two years of house arrest, instead of prison time, for a second felony conviction. That was a tremendous blessing because it helped me get back to discipline, structure, and building a relationship with my children.

That was my life: work, children, recovery meetings. I was building a new life. I knew I could not go back to my children's father and the old way of doing things. Once again, women helped me see my way. My grandmother, of course, but also two of the female rehab counselors, Ola Mae Jones and Rutha Carter, took me under their wings. They encouraged me and nurtured my spirit. For the first time, I began to truly see the impact of women helping women. When these women began to remind me that God wanted more from me, I started to see that I could have something more than what I had been settling for in all this.

***

My grandparents raised me as an only child. My mom and dad were 15 and 16 respectively, when they had me, so my grandparents took me when I was two days old. I am so grateful that I was born during the era when Black families informally adopted. A child going into state custody was unheard of in those days. It was a common practice that a family member would raise the child of a young relative who was not in a position to take care of her own. My grandmother Agnes and grandfather Ike adored me. Their way of expressing love was to make sure I had more than enough. They worked hard to give me a good education. In fact, they both worked as pressers in a laundry, but they always talked about me being educated. I remember teaching my grandfather how to do algebra. We lived a block away from the New Mount Olive Baptist Church of Fort Lauderdale, a place that was perceived as a church for the educated. That's where my grandmother sent me. Education wasn't always easy for me, because a teacher told my grandmother when I was in the third grade that I had some type of learning disorder and would never learn how to read. At reading time she would put me in the corner with a box of crayons to color while the other children read. She refused to try to teach me to read.

"Ignore her," my grandmother said. "With God, all things are possible."

As has always been the case in my life, a woman helped me. My grandmother enlisted the aid of a woman named June Chisholm who patiently taught me how to read.

When I went into recovery, I knew I needed to finish my degree. My grandmother and other women had invested too much in me not to do so. It was a five-year struggle. I was very afraid of going back to school. I had a serious case of the "I can'ts." A woman spoke up for me during the application process at vocational rehabilitation, advocating for me to get the opportunity to go back to school. I had taken an IQ test that indicated that one side of my brain was dead. Under her advocacy, I was allowed to take one class, under one condition: I had to earn at least a C. I took that class and never looked back. I've since earned several other degrees, including a Master's of Divinity from New Orleans Southern Baptist Theological Seminary and a Master's and doctoral degrees in public administration from Nova Southeastern University

(NSU). I am now an adjunct professor at NSU teaching in the Masters of Public Administration Program. All things are possible through Jesus Christ.

Women believed in me until I could believe in myself.

That is why I fiercely believe in women reaching women.

The world has lied to us. We are constantly told that women can't get along. Television shows are built based on this idea. Songs lament — or celebrate — the notion. Books exploit the concept. We've been fed it so often that many of us believe it. I often hear young women say, "Oh, I just can't get along with other females. All of my friends are guys."

These young women have begun to think that they cannot have happy and healthy relationships with other women. It saddens me when women think like that because other women can be some of your best friends and strongest supporters, if you allow them to be. Women can get along. I have built a network of women across this country. No matter where I go in the United States, there is a woman I can call. Whether I need her to bring me panty hose or chicken or to help me find my destination, there is a sister I can depend on there.

But it's not enough that we are made to fear, distrust, and dislike each other. Women are also victims of a hierarchical power system based on disempowerment. This system overlooks our humanity, calls into question our intellect, and places little value on our persons.

Even today, we are forced to survive in the oppressive parallel systems of patriotism and imperialism. On a national level, we don't have all the rights of men — we still earn 77 cents for every dollar a man earns. And on an interpersonal level, we aren't given the same freedoms as men in our relationships. Duality seems to be the order of the day, as one set of forgiving rules governs men and another, more restrictive set, governs women. Don't believe me? Think about this easy example: An aggressive man who states what he wants and goes for it is seen as a stud, a hero, someone to be admired. A woman who does the same thing is seen in much less favorable terms, often being referred to as out of order or bossy.

These systematic principalities bring a lot of heat to our

lives as we struggle to be "more excellent" sisters, mothers, wives, and disciples.

In spite of institutionalized systems of oppression, God is calling women to reach women. Women are hungering and thirsting for God — whether they are saved or un-churched. Women must educate, empower, and equip each other. As God pours out the Spirit of Christ — the Holy Spirit — that is within us, through sisterly sharing and caring, this world will be transformed.

The institutionalized systems of oppression have produced the crisis in which we find ourselves today. Healthwise, we are being infected with HIV at an alarming rate. In some communities, we are dying from preventable illnesses. Financially, our earning never quite catches up to that of men and we are forever living on the edge, just one disaster away from homelessness. Educationally, we are outpacing men, but the result is we then find ourselves with no one to date when we seek companionship.

When we realize this, we can change it. It all starts with how we view our lives and the events going on in them.

I used to view my life from a worldly perspective. I made decisions based on what society told me was good. Today, I have a new psyche or a renewing of the mind. Now, I make decisions based on what God tells me is good. The reason this is important is because society will cause me to doubt my relationships with women and even to avoid them. But God tells me to cherish, embrace, and celebrate those relationships. When we live subjected to the Holy Spirit, we see life from a spiritual perspective.

The outpouring of the Holy Spirit chases away the petty differences and silly arguments that separate us. Why is it that we battle each other over matters of pure choice? One such perennial battle is the one over taking care of a family. Women who have the option to stay home and raise their children see their work as more important and more worthy than the work of mothers who earn a living outside the home. Mothers who work outside the home feel they have it tougher than their sisters who do stay home, and each side looks a little distrustfully at the other. This is a petty argument designed by Satan to keep us from unifying. The reality is that motherhood comes in a variety of shades. Your approach to it may be different from mine. It doesn't mean either of us loves our children any less.

Another argument that often separates women is that of breastfeeding. Breastfeeding mothers look down on mothers who rely on a bottle, while bottle-feeding mothers feel a bit put-upon by their breastfeeding sisters. As with the previous argument, both sides put pressure on the other. They judge each other based on the choice to breastfeed or not. This argument, like the previous one, is designed to separate. Rather than judging each other based on how we feed a baby, we must embrace each other and show support, realizing that taking care of a child is a tough job, no matter what.

We can't get through the very real crisis we are facing if we continue to pit ourselves one against the other. Overcoming centuries of gender inequality and decades of discrimination will take us intentionally reaching out to one another.

Acts. 1:8 tells us to share the gospel to the ends of the earth. Women reaching women is not just a socially conscious movement. It is a direct command from God. Women need to understand that God can lift them from crisis. Sisters need to know they are not alone as they are battling depression, battling cancer or as they are going through divorce. A sister needs to know that her baggage doesn't have to define her life. She can be relieved from the burdens of life. God cares about her personal crises.

Some may decry the use of the word "crisis," feeling that women have always faced tough times. They may say today's woman is no worse off than women of a generation ago or Biblical times or any other period.

I disagree. Today's woman faces a crisis like never before because of the very nature of the pressures that dominate her life. She simply does not have the sense of sisterhood that used to be commonplace. Women in Biblical times, for instance, often did most of their tasks in groups. They cooked together, raised children together, tended chores together. Women even a generation ago had more interaction because women's groups, social clubs, and communities were more prevalent.

Today, women are more isolated, which means they face more of their pressures on their own. As connected as the Internet makes the world, it is almost a bit of a double-edged sword because it can also isolate women who previously had to go out to do certain tasks. Now, a woman can go for a week or more without stepping foot out the door. She can work from home, go to school from home, shop from home.

And in all this, she can go for days without ever having a traditional conversation with another woman.

WOMEN REACHING WOMEN MOMENT

We can shy away from sharing our faith in settings outside of church. When we are at work, in school, in the grocery store, or even at family gatherings, we may remain silent when it comes to faith for fear of offending others. But sharing your faith can help to reach another woman. Look for ways to share your faith this week and reach out to other women at the same time.

"Even though I walk through the darkest valley, I will fear no evil, for you are with me; your rod and your staff, they comfort me." – Psalm 23:4

2 Sisterhood Uplifts, Heals Wounds

For many women the church is the last house on the block. After being used, abused, and misused they go to the church seeking refuge. They seek healing for their weary, wounded and wanting minds, bodies, and souls. Deception, demoralization, and disease have wrecked havoc, but they turn to the church as their last hope.

That is why I believe in the multigenerational approach. Using a broad one-size-fits-all approach quit working when we traded the slow cooker for the microwave. In fact, it has never really worked. In many congregations today, women are in cliques or gangs. Yes, gangs in the church. To be frank, the gangs rival each other. Oftentimes, the gang leader —or ministry leader, to use a nice spiritual term — has influenced members negatively. There are constant turf battles in which the concept of Kingdom is lost. Instead of unity, we find division. The result is that many women never build relationships outside the clique. So the women who have come to church to find help, sometimes still find hurt.

Twenty-first Century churches must be effectively equipped to meet the needs of hurting women. In this moment we need a multigenerational approach to women's ministry. Women's ministries must be multigenerational, multidenominational, and multicultural. Pain doesn't come only in one age, denomination, or race.

I am convinced that a multigenerational approach based on the Titus 2:3-5 model will meet the needs of all women. It reads: "Likewise, teach the older women to be reverent in the way they live, not to be slanderers or addicted to much wine, but to teach what is good. Then they can urge the younger women to love their husbands and children, to be self-controlled and pure, to be busy at home, to be kind, and to be subject to their husbands, so that no one will malign the word of God."

***

This model is clear about older women training younger women. Women's ministry must be intentionally designed to accommodate the fact that women seek different things from church at different ages. Our churches are comprised of distinctive age groups. The Builders, those ages 65-85, are looking for stability. They aren't interested in a whole lot of change. They want something that is routine. Their worship services, their ministries, and their events must provide this.

The Boomers, those ages 45-65, are looking for quality. They are at a point in life where it's not enough just to have something. They want it to be nice. So whatever you do for them can't be done haphazardly. It must have value and substance.

The Busters, age 25-45, are looking for simplicity. They're not interested in a lot of tradition or stuffiness. They want an experience that is free flowing, open, and inviting.

The Bridgers, age 25 and younger, are looking for community or a sense of belonging. Fitting in is the most important thing to this group. They like to do what their friends are doing, so any experience you are creating for them must have the support of a large number of those in this age group. They want to be a part of something cool.

***

You can see from the descriptions of each age group that their interests are not necessarily the same as those of women in another group. Your 25-year-old, for instance, is not going to be attracted to the same types of activities as a 65-year-old. One wants tradition and stability. The other wants something simple, new, and open. The wisdom that I have gained from sitting at the skirt tales of older women has added value to my life. I could not acquire such wisdom from a classroom textbook.

I like to host Living Legend Teas. These events are designed to create an environment for women over 70 to share their wisdom. I ask each legend to be a panel member and respond to the questions of younger women in the audience.

"A mother must be committed to raising her children and responding to the needs of her husband," Mother Pettis told us one year. Her comment has stayed with me.

Her children have done well in life. One son is a very prominent lawyer. Another is a renowned dentist. Both sons own their practices and several daughters are positive role models as well.

I also remember the many stories of Mother Louise Mann.

Mother Mann left an abusive marriage and raised her two sons alone. She constantly talks about working hard and making a difference in one's community. Mother Mann marched with the local NAACP in the sixties and seventies. Over the past twenty years she has served more than 5,000 families through an annual Thanksgiving basket drive and Angel Tree project, which sees hundreds of volunteers provide food, clothing, and toys to less fortunate families. Today, at 83, she runs a nutrition site for seniors four days a week. She is known all over the country for her missionary efforts at home and abroad. Mother Mann's generosity has touched even my family, as she made sure I had enough food to feed my babies when I left the streets and returned to the church in 1990. She also got me involved with the Matrons Ministry at our church. Mother Mann and Mother Pettis are just two of the many seasoned women whose love has blessed my life. So I know from personal experience that the care, interest, and guidance of mature women can help younger women navigate life. These women reached out and addressed the specific needs they saw.

If we address their specific needs, we will find our churches able to retain more women, because those women will be happier and more fulfilled overall. This is important to the health and life of any church. A church cannot be vibrant and growing if its membership is shrinking. If all of its members are leaving or participating less and less, then that church will soon cease to be relevant. We must design ministries that are interesting, engaging, and accommodating for all women.

In addition to the programmatic needs, we must address the emotional needs of women in churches. No matter how pretty they look or how put-together they sound, women are in distress in every congregation. It doesn't matter the socio-economic level of the church or its community. This is a universal truth, I have found. Distress knows no bounds. Women in congregations all over the world are in LoDebar. The Biblical place of LoDebar was without greenery. It was dry and barren. LoDebar was a desolate place with absolutely no growth potential. I liken that Biblical place to a spiritual place we find ourselves in today when church becomes a masquerade party. We wear our masks and the best hair, whether it is Remy, a lace front wig, or our own. We use the outside to hide the turmoil on the inside.

As a matter of fact, every woman, as a result of the fall in the Garden of Eden, has an element of hurt or pain. She finds herself in LoDebar at some point. In LoDebar, a place of nothing, you become emotionally bankrupt. In LoDebar, you internalize your injury so that not only are you injured, you become your injury. And the enemy is using that to keep us lame and crippled.

But God says all things work together for the good and the thing that happened to you that was so terrible doesn't have to maintain its painful grip over your life. God can turn that terrible thing into a testimony. Sisters, if you take nothing else from this book, please take that: God can turn that terrible thing that happened to you into a testimony. The abuse. The rape. The beating. The neglect. The financial ruin. The estrangement from a loved one. The disease. Yes, even the thing you've never told anyone else about, even that. God can turn every bad thing you've endured into a testimony. That testimony can be your story of how God helped you to overcome. There is always a story behind the story.

I know it may not seem possible now, as tears stream down your face and hurt tightens your chest, but you can release the hurt and be free to live again. God can restore your heart. Please believe me, sister. The Bible says in Revelation 12:11 we overcome by the blood of Jesus and by the power of our testimony.

When God created Adam, He created him perfectly. But then came sin. Sin is the root of pain and suffering. But somewhere along the journey, we can move from being injured to being a force for God — if we make ourselves available through Jesus Christ.

That is the beauty of our Christian walk. God has created us to testify, to evangelize, and to be proponents of prophetic ministry. Luke confirms this as he quotes the minor prophet Joel in Acts 2:18: "Even on my servants, both men and women, I will pour out my Spirit in those days, and they will prophesy."

Every woman has a word inside of her about Jesus. Her womb is pregnant with potential. When she invites Christ into her life, that intimacy with Him revolutionizes her future. So what the enemy thought would kill her — that rape, that prostitution, that drug addiction — was actually pushing her into her purpose. And that purpose is to give God glory. Sister, others may discard you like trash or tell you you'll never be anything because of where you've been, but God knows where you've been and He is longing to help you reach a place you've never imagined you could be. He is able to do exceedingly and abundantly above anything that you could ever think or ask. What I so love about Him is that there is nothing that you or I could do that would make God give up on us. There is nothing that you or I could do that would make God give us up.

We can give God glory in so many wonderful ways. Whether I give Him glory through preaching or showing up at a hospital to rock a crack baby or by lending a kind word to another in need, I am witnessing. I witness through my daily life. The same is for you. Each action you take is a witness. You get to decide what kind of witness you bear.

I know a woman who had her first baby at 12 but she is a Harvard graduate. She did not let her past define her future. It merely became an opportunity for her to testify about the glory of God. Many people would expect a teen mother to become another statistic — no education, no prospects, no future. But that young lady is here to say, "With God's help, we can all write a story different from what others try to write for us."

Yes, through our pain, God pushes us into our purpose. At one point, I could not see my way up. I was in the dark cave of life. Addiction had me bound. But that is not where my story ends. The pain of drug abuse, incarceration, and poor choices was preparation for my Kingdom assignment that I am living out today.

When we embrace each other in sisterhood, we become each other's burden barriers. We become a support system for each other.

We each become part of the other's testimony. Each sister who reaches out to another sister helps fulfill her own purpose while simultaneously helping her sister fulfill hers.

***

Women are lonely without each other.

We have to reach women because right now we are outliving the men. We can't lean only on our men, expecting them to carry us through life. Instead, women must form strong, meaningful relationships that take us from life event to life event, from youth through old age. If women come together, we will be like the church in the book of Acts. When they got on one accord, miracles literally took place.

When women get on one accord, we can transform the world. We can have an impact that lasts for generations. History has always been witness to women doing great and mighty things, but that same history has not always acknowledged those deeds. However, I can bring to your attention a few women right off who did deeds that helped shape history. When you look at Harriet Tubman, who knew she was created to be nobody's slave; Ida B. Wells-Barnett, who said no to unequal rights; and Mary McCloud Bethune, who realized Negro girls needed an education; you see the potential to do great things. If you think about it, I'm sure you can come up with your own list of women who have touched lives in a powerful way.

How is it that women are able to have such an impact? Well, I think women have been built to last. We were made to be strong, and conditioned to be tough. While we can cite strong women all the way back to Biblical times, I point now to the recent history of slavery as a factor that has impacted the strength of Black women in particular.

The Black woman worked harder than anybody else. She had to work in the field, in the house, and of course, in the bedroom. She was the one tasked with the regular work of the day, plus accommodating the roving eye of the property owner, while coping with the loss of her children as they were sold off to the highest bidder. Through the pain and agony of all this, she didn't lose her mind. Something inside of her kept her mind and soul together and helped her to become strong.

Women in America have had to fight for their right to be heard in the voting booth, and for their work to be worth the same as a man's for doing the same job. The fight to be heard continues for many women around the world, and even right here in the United States, the struggle for equal pay goes on — yes, even today.

I believe that when God created women, we were uniquely and wonderfully made. God put Adam under Divine Anesthesia. While Adam was out God reached into Adam's side and pulled out a rib and formed woman. He gave us curves and shapes to show off his architectural skills. He gave us a womb because He wanted to impregnate us with natural and spiritual purpose. Even after the fall in the Garden He blessed us with the innate ability to identify and call out the enemy. I will explore this in a future book.

When we coast through our lives with no regard for purpose, we turn our backs on God's plan for us. We ignore the huge potential He has placed within our wombs and we choose merely to exist, not to live.

When women come together and connect in the spirit in prayer, praise, and proclamation, we see results. I witness this often. I began a morning conference call, the Women Reaching Women Word Network, to bring together women from all walks of life some time back. That network has been the place of many sermons, testimonies, prayers, and heartfelt moments. It also has been the place of support, encouragement, and miracles, as women have been strengthened, delivered and have seen prayers answered in a mighty way.

Now is the time for you, sister, to connect with other sisters and call on God's name for a great purpose. And don't think you must start out with something grand or even a multitude of people. Just start by reaching out to one sister. Encourage her. Support her. Pray with and for her. And let her do the same for you. So, what will you and your sister unite to do? What blessing will you pray for in the name of Jesus for your sister? What blessing will you ask her to request on your behalf? Remember, Jesus said in Matthew 18:20, "For where two or three gather in my name, there am I with them."

***

Women need each other now more than ever.

Women have made tremendous strides over the past 100

years. We've become more independent, more educated, and more financially free than ever before. A woman used to need a man simply to be able to live — a man had to protect her, give her shelter, even own the property her father passed down. Ecclesiastes 3 tells us there is a time and a season for everything. And women, it is our season! As my spiritual daughter, Pastor Toni Charles would say, it is our "Kairos, moment." It is our supreme moment. Although we are more autonomous than ever before, we cannot let our independence make us forget the struggles that led us to this point, nor can we allow them to make us forget the sisters who helped us arrive here.

Because we are so independent, we are also seeing another effect: We are often single. Of course, it's no secret that women tend to outlive men. So right off, women must prepare for a life when a man is not there. But even outside of marriages and long-term relationships that end in death, many marriages end in divorce. With our increasing independence, we are finding that we no longer have to stay in untenable situations like our sisters did in the past. We can choose to leave abusive, dead, and decaying relationships. Another reason for our singleness is that sometimes find no eligible bachelors as we climb the ladder to accomplishment. Not wanting to settle for anything less than what God has for us, we choose to remain on our own. All of these reasons increase the urgency of my message. We must embrace each other. Aside from God, sometimes, we're all we have. God has placed me in the 21st Century for a time such as this. Yes, it is our own personal reality show. Every day we live, we are writing a paragraph. Every month is writing a chapter. Every year is writing a book. We truly are living out the days of our lives. Some of us are young and restless, others are desperate housewives and others are just living minute by minute as the world turns. We have an obligation to leave a legacy. God has invited us to be a part of a bigger story. This book process is another part of me leaving a legacy. I hope that when I die, there will be at least three or four women who stand up and say I influenced their lives positively. I want the same for you, as well.

Time out for competition amongst us sisters. The work

God has for us is too important for that. Let's inspire each other to live with purpose.

WOMEN REACHING WOMEN MOMENT

List five ways your life has been positively impacted by women. What did you learn from each of these women?

"A wife of noble character who can find? She is worth far more than rubies." – Proverbs 31: 10

3 Biblical Stories Relevant Even to This Day

I find a lot of value in the lives of women of the Bible. Their stories are often told through our pastors or our male clergy. Not to diminish their work, but a lot of times they don't do the due diligence it will take to tell the stories in a way that has meaning for today's women. That's why I think it's important for us as women to study the stories of women in the Bible.

That is part of my gift: God allows me to see through the lives of those women in a very unique way to minister to women today.

That's important because we often look at stories of the Bible and think they are just cute tales, but they were only relevant to that time. We can't see how they apply to our lives today, more than 2000 years later. For this reason, many sisters avoid reading the Bible or read it only in a superficial way. But I believe when you are able to relate many of the Bible's stories to your current circumstances, you will gain new revelation as you suddenly see that what women all those years ago dealt with can help you through your situation today.

Consider the contemporary application of many of the Biblical messages.

Hannah: Baby Mama Drama

1 Samuel 1:1-20

Hannah cannot bear children. So the very thing that makes her a woman has been shut off. In 1 Samuel 1:6, we see God closed her womb. So the very essence of who she is has been affected. God created women to give birth. We know in ancient Hebrew times, a woman's value was tied to her husband and her ability to bear children.

So if you were not able to have children, it meant something was wrong with you. You were ostracized. You had a lower status.

As a result of societal pressure, Hannah feels pretty sad at times. I say her husband Elkanah is a very bipolar man, because on the one hand, we see him being a faithful worshipper. But on the other hand, we see him hanging out with Eli's two wicked sons, Hophni and Phineas, who were womanizers. I believe his association with the boys escalated his desire to have Peninnah. So his inability to withstand peer pressure makes his family dysfunctional.

We see Hannah clearly dealing with baby mama drama because Elkanah takes Peninnah to be his wife and she has children for him. Peninnah holds this over Hannah. Every chance she gets, she picks at Hannah and makes fun of the fact that the woman is barren.

She is so hateful in her insults that Hannah cries and takes to her bed and does not eat.

In 1 Samuel 1:8, we find out her husband's response: "Hannah, why are you weeping? Why don't you eat? Why are you downhearted? Don't I mean more to you than ten sons?"

You see, even in Biblical times, men had giant egos. Elkanah asked her something only a man would: "Don't I mean more to you than ten sons?" As far as he was concerned, he was all Hannah needed.

Imagine Hannah is sitting there. Her womb is closed. Her husband's cackling mistress is talking trash. Her conceited husband asks her, "Am I not better than ten men? Am I not all you need?" The one person she needs to understand where she is coming from can't grasp her pain. He doesn't put the other woman in check.

In fact, once a year they all go to Shiloh, a place of tranquility, to worship. Hannah, her husband, his babies' mama, and the outside kids, all sit at the dinner table. No wonder Hannah is so overwhelmed she cannot even eat.

Let's be honest sisters. Most of us would have laid ungodly hands on Peninnah.

But that kind of pressure pushes Hannah into prayer. Sometimes the pains of life push us into prayer, push us into the presence of God. It's during these desperate times that the Holy Spirit deals with us. I've certainly found myself in this place a time or two. I've been in such bad shape that all I could do was cry out to God.

When I finally made the decision to leave drugs behind, I had to lean on God as I grew in recovery. When I was diagnosed with cancer in 2005, I had to lean on God even more. When I went through my last divorce, I had to lean on God. When I've faced financial difficulties or have had other struggles, I've had to lean on God.

The tornadoes, storms, and hurricanes of life were trying to huff and puff and blow me away. But the Captain of the ship heard my despairing cry and He rescued me. I can truthfully say that each time I turned to God in desperation, He delivered. I believe God in His permissive will allows us to reach such a low sometime where we must rely solely on Him. I echo the words of the Psalmist, " My help comes from the Lord, who made the heaven and earth. He will not allow my foot to slip; He who keeps me will not slumber. He is my source."

So when Hannah is crying out in this scripture, you must understand that she is at her rock bottom. Nothing is going right for her. Pain has rendered her unable to function. She isn't trying to argue with her husband's baby mama and she isn't trying to make her husband tell that woman to leave her alone. She isn't even trying to refute the gossip about why she is not able to get pregnant.

In Hannah's spirit the old hymn of the church begins to resonate: " Oh what a friend we have in Jesus, all our sins and griefs to bare; oh what a privilege it is to carry every thing to God in prayer."

Hannah gets up off her pity pot and makes her way to a place where she can have a little talk with Jesus.

You know when you have emotional pain and mental pain it leads to physical pain. Maybe her stomach has started to tie itself in knots and hurt or her head is throbbing. Whatever it is, Hannah is at her worst.

And that is where she meets God.

She goes to the Lord's temple and just travail in prayer. This is a prayer where the words bubble up in her gut and her mouth moves, but no sound comes from her lips. She is praying inside, where all the hurt is.

This is a prayer with snot running out of her nose, tears running out of her eyes, all in the presence of God. The scene reminds me of another old spiritual, "It's not my mother or my father but it is Me, Oh Lord standing in the need of prayer." As I lean to my spiritual imagination to set the scene here, I imagine Hannah shaking her head and putting her hand to her chest.

Her eyes are blurry and her tears make it hard to see. She cries inwardly, "I'm on the verge of a breakdown," she pleads. "I am about to lose my mind. I need a miracle from you, and I need it now."

She never opens her mouth but the issues of her heart flow. She casts her cares on God. Her situation actually gets worst. She is praying in such a way that Eli the priest accuses her of being drunk. That's right. The Pastor is observing at the door and accuses her of being drunk. But she isn't drunk. She is just a woman life has hurt so badly that she has a sorrowful spirit.

I asked myself why didn't Hannah ask the man of God to pray for her or with her. I believe Hannah feels that nobody can express her pain to God like she can. She is a woman whose pain has pushed her into prayer and then into purpose.

The story behind the story suggests that Hannah is a sister who has been through depression, devastation, and desperation. Hannah has landed on her knees in the presence of God. God has protected her mind, her body, and her spirit. Through her crying out, she realizes she has been preserved for purpose.

She promises God that if He would just manifest her purpose in the earth by giving her a son, she will dedicate that child to God's work.

And immediately her face is no longer sad and by the end of the year, she has her baby!

The barren woman whose husband has taken another woman to give him children has been released from the curse of a closed womb. She is released from it when she cries out to God and depends on Him. In actuality nobody else, not Elkanah, not Peninnah, not Eli could have relieved Hannah's pain. Baby mama drama sent her to the Lord.

But you know how God shows up and shows out. As Ephesians 3:20 tells us, He can do more than we can even ask or think, according to His power within us. He can bless us abundantly, in ways that will blow our minds! And God does this for Hannah. Not only does He give her Samuel, whom she dedicates to the Lord and sends to live at the temple, He blesses her with three more sons and two daughters! Remember Samuel is not just any kid. He goes down in history as being the one who anoints.

Now, that is some blessing!

For a woman who for years has tried to get pregnant but cannot to suddenly have six children, you know it is nobody but God. He is a God of overflow.

How can you apply this Biblical story to life today? Well, for starters, if you are dealing with some baby mama drama nonsense, know there is hope. Your situation can change. It doesn't always have to be the way it is today. If your man has stepped out on you and has gotten another woman pregnant, you can use Hannah's example. How? She went to God to help her solve her issue. So you can do the same.

You don't have to fight the situation with your fists. All you have to do is clothe yourself right as Paul says in his letter to the Romans. Each morning you must put on the whole armor of God. Protect your mind with the helmet of salvation. Put on the breastplate of righteousness to guard your heart and all the other major organs.

Gird your waist with truth.

Put on your Gospel pumps that bring peace. Take your shield of faith in one hand and your sword of the spirit, which is the word of God, in the other. After you are dressed then put on the overcoat of prayer to ignite the armor.

Prayer gives power to the armor and you will be able to stand against the wiles of the devil. In many instances you won't even have to say or do anything to the enemy.

As with Hannah, God will fix the situation. He will move supernaturally and the fiery darts of those who seek to harm you will no longer affect you in anyway. This is what happened in Hannah's case. Peninnah, the clean-up woman, was picking at her for one reason: Hannah couldn't have children. Peninnah literally made herself feel good at Hannah's expense.

So God fixed it to where that was no longer an issue. Suddenly Peninnah's hold over Hannah was released.

In today's times, you might find that you are constantly being harassed by a baby mama drama situation. Maybe the hurt from the betrayal is weighing on you so much that, like Hannah, you can't even eat. If so, then take comfort and know that God can heal your heart and make this not even be an issue for you.

Through your prayers, you can find the strength and guidance to handle your baby mama drama. Psalm 37:1-4 says "Do not fret because of those who are evil or be envious of those who do wrong; for like the grass they will soon wither, like green plants they will soon die away. Trust in the Lord and do good; dwell in the land and enjoy safe pasture. Take the delight in the Lord, and he will give you the desires of your heart."

***

When I look at my life and all I have gone through — the drugs and alcohol, the divorces, the cancer — I know I shouldn't even be alive but God has preserved me for purpose. So I gain strength from Hannah's story. Hannah's ability to stay in the presence of God ultimately allowed her to end up receiving the promises of God.

We have to understand there is a road map from pain to promise.

Out of your pain you birth your purpose and in your purpose you experience God's promises. Are you willing to push in prayer? It will allow you to move beyond your pain and receive the promises that God has just for you.

I'd like to explore one other point before we move from Hannah's story. Hannah — or Anna — in Hebrew, means grace. So it means she had the favor of God. When we look at our lives, we often can't see the favor of God. The enemy wants us to believe God doesn't love us, but some of that pain is God's way of making and molding us into who we are destined to be.

When I travel around the country and meet women who were molested at 7 and other women who have experienced physical abuse for years, I reflect on my own personal challenges. The question becomes: "Why are we still here?" The answer is the same as I mentioned earlier: We are here because we are built to last, sisters. So your pain doesn't define you; it refines your testimony.

That is what happened to Hannah. If we move on to the second chapter, we find that Hannah's pleading, painful prayer of the first chapter has now become a prayer that turns into a beautiful song. In 1 Samuel 2:1-10, Hannah rejoices at having been blessed with an unexpected child.

The thing that is stressing you out now can turn into an unimaginable blessing later. Just pray and trust God.

Canaanite Woman with Demon-Possessed Daughter: Operating in Obscurity

Before I get into the pertinent details of the Canaanite woman's story I believe that a discussion of the characteristics of her people can be beneficial.

Judges 2:18-19 says, "Whenever the LORD raised up a judge for them, he was with the judge and saved them out of the hands of their enemies as long as the judge lived; for the LORD had relented because of their groaning under those who oppressed and afflicted them. But when the judge died, the people returned to ways even more corrupt than those of their ancestors, following other gods and serving and worshiping them. They refused to give up their evil practices and stubborn ways."

In these two verses we find the pattern for the entire book of Judges — a pattern of sin, bondage, and repentance that lasts for nearly 350 years (around 1380 to 1050 BC). We can see such a cycle of sin in many of our lives, even today. The cycle happens when we repeat the same mistakes over and over. We may have brief moments where it looks like we've overcome the tendency to commit those sins, but they find a way to show up again.

When we're in that cycle of sin, we sometimes believe we have gotten control of it, but suddenly, we find ourselves back in the same spot.

Such is the history of the Israelites and the Canaanites. The Canaanites are toxic bullies. People go out of their way to avoid travel routes where they can run into the Canaanites, who control many of the highways. Living in many unprotected villages is unsafe for the Israelites.

The Israelites are drawn into observing many of the customs of the Cananites, including worshipping their gods. As they step away from God and fall under the influence of the Canaanites, they find themselves at war again.

The Israelites let themselves be influenced by the Canaanites. Because of their inability to live by what they know to be right and to stand for their own beliefs, their spirits are corrupted. The bad habits of their Canaanite neighbors rub off on them.

We can learn much from the Israelites' plight. They let peer pressure from toxic people push them into poor behavior. How often does that happen to us? When we learn to identify people who are toxic, we can be prepared to stand against them. We don't have to feel powerless against their influence. We don't have to keep making the same mistakes.

Like the Israelites, when we are stuck in a cycle of sin, we can also feel despair as we recognize we are unable to fix the problem by ourselves. I am thankful for the Apostle Paul because he too struggled with the vicious cycle of his sinful nature. He says in Romans 7:19, "For I do not do the good I want to do, but the evil I do not want to do — this I keep doing."

Matthew 15:21-28

A Canaanite woman hears about Jesus and the miracles He has performed. She is desperate for a miracle because an evil spirit has taken over her daughter. It's likely that she is being blamed for her daughter's condition. Her neighbors are convinced that her sin has caused her daughter to be possessed by a demonic spirit.

Whether this is true or not, we see this Canaanite woman goes against traditional culture. She is so desperate, in fact, that she interrupts a meeting Jesus is having with the disciples.

Let me set the scene for you. For this woman, there is no pastor to cure her daughter. She can't write a check to get access to proper treatment for her child. She's tried all the local people who claim to be able to help, but still her daughter has a demon inside. So this woman goes into the meeting Jesus is having. He has just left Galilee and has matriculated to the pagan region of Tyre and Sidon in Phoenicia, which is modern day Lebanon, to get away from the drama of the Jewish church leaders.

Keep in mind that Jesus' reputation precedes Him. Jesus has walked on the water without getting His feet wet. He showed up at Lake Gennesaret and all the sick people who touched the hem of His garment were healed.

He has now withdrawn to this pagan land to take a little break when this Canaanite woman engages Him.

And, as we know, in Biblical times women aren't held in great esteem anyway. The fact that she is interrupting a meeting, and that she is a woman, already has the deck stacked against her. Add to that, she is a Canaanite. She is a gentile. The Canaanite woman is from one of the seven nations driven out of the land of Canaan in the Old Testament. Her people worship idol gods. They sacrifice children and do all types of other ungodly things. They and the Jews are bitter enemies, ancestral enemies.

The Jews often refer to them as dogs and consider them to be unclean. The Jews and the Canaanites hate each other.

This woman begins to operate in obscurity. Obscurity is when you don't understand what's going on. Your way seems dark. Even your theology is in a crisis because what God is permitting to happen in your life is obscured. Maze featuring Frankie Beverly sings about these times in "Joy and Pain." When the group likens joy and pain to sunshine and rain, you get the picture.

Both the good and bad are all wrapped in together, causing you to have some serious issues. One minute you are laughing, the next minute you are crying. Life is dark and cloudy. You are confused.

Life is ambiguous. You have no answers but you must be able to operate. The various roles that you play demand that you operate in spite of your emotions, in spite of your physical and even spiritual state. As a matter of fact, lives depend on you being able to operate. If you are a Christian, souls depend on you being able to operate.

To people of her time, the Canaanite woman is less than a nobody. She is not someone anyone else would give the time of day. So a woman who is able to operate in obscurity must be able to do so in the face of persistent problems. When you look at the text and she asks Jesus for help, He first ignores her. Then the disciples basically say throw her out.

So this is a woman who is looked down upon by society, and the Healer she goes to see seems not to want to have anything to do with her. His crew is certainly hostile. Even those around her turn their noses up at her, as they wonder what she did to cause this affliction. After all, their daughters aren't demon-possessed, so why is hers?

She definitely has persistent problems. In today's language, we would say she was from the wrong side of the tracks. And it went downhill from there. The disciples, the men of God who have been called to serve, are the ones turning on her. They are the ones calling for her to be thrown out of the meeting. They are behaving like pitiful people.

In this context, I call the disciples hope bandits, because they are trying to steal her optimism. But she doesn't let the hope bandits snatch it. Women must be able to operate in the midst of pitiful people.

Pitiful people will try to snatch your hope. They will try to block your blessings. Instead, in verse 25 she gets on her knees before Jesus. She takes her prayer game to a whole other level. She says, Lord please.

She is not going to leave until she gets what she wants. Even then, her request is not granted. Instead, Jesus, who has at first ignored her, now uses the Greek word Kunarios, which means little dog or house dog.

Basically, what Jesus is doing is checking her: "Are you able to handle the fact that you are from a bad pedigree? Can you handle the fact that you are a woman in a man's world trying to get a blessing? Will you give up? How bad do you want it? "

He wants to see whether she will persist in the face of opposition. This sister hangs in there. She refuses to quit. She says even dogs get crumbs from the master's table.

And so Jesus grants her request. Her daughter is healed. Why? Because even as she operates in obscurity, even as she faces down those who oppose her, even as she takes insults, she remains steadfast in her trust in the Almighty Healer.

Sisters, we can all take a lesson from this woman. We may operate in obscurity and others may say we are worthless or from the "wrong" side of the tracks. But if we believe in the power of God, we must persevere anyway.

And when we meet opposition, like this woman, we must find a way to face it. Opposition should not automatically be a sign to give up. It could be God testing our faith. And if we immediately turn and run away, what does that say about that faith?

That Canaanite woman came for a miracle, and she was not leaving until she got it. She was focused and willing to take the grief that came to her. A lot of times when people run their mouths on us, it causes us to stop going to church or to quit jobs. It poisons our spirits and we find ourselves being incapacitated. If we are going to operate in today's world, we must be willing to trust God.

Jesus healed the Canaanite woman's daughter, even when nothing else worked. When we are facing a dire diagnosis and a poor prognosis, God can still work a miracle for us. God is not limited by man's inability to create a desired result.

So what else can we take from this woman's story? Well, in life we will encounter various types of hope bandits. We will encounter alarmists who are quick to broadcast anything that is wrong. We will encounter critics who are happy to evaluate every angle of us — our job, our life, our ministry. This is normally a self appointed position with no anointing.

We will encounter the cynic, the person who tries to sap our hope because he is so focused on saying what can't be. We will encounter the contrarian, a cousin of the cynic. This person is ready to naysay anything we say, no matter what. This is the person who is constantly trying to choke the hope out of us. But through it all, we have to be hope managers, cultivators of hope, just as this woman was. She was able to operate in spite of persisting problems, pitiful people, and petty pontification.

Woman at the Well: Sordid past

John 4:7-30

Jesus is traveling with his disciples when he stops at Jacob's Well in Samaria. The disciples go into town to get food but Jesus, tired from the journey, stays behind. About noon, a Samaritan woman approaches. She likes to show up at this time, in the heat of the day, so she doesn't bump into anyone she knows. She's a bit of an outcast because she's been with a lot of men. She is the cleanup woman. She is the sister that all women hate. She is the around-the-way girl. Life has convinced her that being a sex object adds value to her character.

Jesus asks her for some water and she does a double-take. John 4:9 says, "The Samaritan woman said to Him, 'You are a Jew and I am a Samaritan woman. How can you ask me for a drink?' (For Jews do not associate with Samaritans.)"

Jesus tells her that really, He has water that will last forever and if she knew who He was, she would ask Him for water. She asks and He says go get your husband, to which she replies that she's not married.

Jesus says, yeah, you're right, you're not married. You've been married five times and the man you're with now is not your husband. The woman thinks Jesus is a prophet when she realizes He knows all about her past. Once she finds out that He is the Messiah, her spirit is renewed, and she goes to town to tell all who will listen about her encounter.

This story behind the story lets us know that God forgives us of our sins, when we ask. Others may ostracize us, like they did this woman, but He does not. It also lets us know that He is the source of life everlasting.

If you've ever been the criticized or looked down on because of your past, then this story will hit home. Sometimes we make so many mistakes in life that we internalize them and begin to feel that we can never get beyond them. Like the woman, we may avoid all that is familiar because we can't take one more snide comment or one more condemning look.

I am always excited when people bring up my past. It gives me another opportunity to brag on God. I usually respond using some words that I have borrowed from the second letter that Paul wrote to Timothy. "I was a blasphemer, an insolent woman. As a matter of fact, I was the chief sinner."

I was worse than all the others. Satan and I had a thing going on. I was a sergeant in Satan's army. Satan used me and used me until he ran me to Jesus. Now that I am in the Lord's army I have gotten a promotion. I am a general. Every day that God wakes me up, Satan knows that he will fight another losing battle. I am on the battlefield for the Lord. I will fight for me and I will fight for you.

A woman with a sordid past is not grounded in the word of God. The social pressure can be wearing and can lead to depression. Jesus lets us know that if we come to Him, He can wipe away even a bad past. And if Jesus can forgive us for what we've done, shouldn't we be willing to forgive our sisters — even those who have committed what we consider to be pretty horrible acts?

The Woman at the Well represents each of us when we are operating in the sin cycles of our life. And her story symbolizes what God will do to make it right.

Esther and Vashti: In the palace for purpose

Book of Esther

Philosopher and theologian Soren Kierkegaard suggests that there are three phases of human existence. In the Aesthetic Stage, people are never satisfied, as they are dominated by physical, emotional, and intellectual desires. In the Ethical Stage, people are consumed with a sense of right and wrong. They choose between equal evil options. The Religious Stage is one that advocates people are Knights of

Infinite Resignation. They are religious but bound by guilt. Or people are Knights of Faith. They live in response to God, regardless of appearance. I believe that the American social system focuses on the Aesthetic Stage, beauty and physique. This creates tension. Women are spending thousands of dollars to be beautiful. Let me be upfront. I think we should be pretty. I am a member of Alpha Kappa Alpha Sorority, Inc., and beauty and brilliance are required for membership. The problem is that what defines beauty continues to change. As women, we have to get to a point where we understand that being pretty is not enough. When we look at the book of Esther, it starts with the story of Vashti. This is a story we often glance right over. We hear that she was a woman who disobeyed her husband and she was put out because of it. But let us study this for a moment, because within this story is a powerful message.

First, let's look at Vashti's lineage. She is the daughter of Babylon's King Belshazzar, an alcoholic, and the great - granddaughter of Nebuchadnezzar, a crazy man who raided the temple.

But not only is she born into royalty, she is beautiful. Even her name actually means most beautiful. She is now the queen, the wife of King Xerxes or Ahasuerus, who rules a large area. And she is so beautiful in fact, King Xerxes calls for her to come dance before him and all of his buddies after his 180-day party to show off his prize catch. He wants everyone to admire this fine woman he calls wife.

Xerxes is following in Vashti's father's footsteps. Her dad, Belshazzar, was known for getting so drunk that he would worship the gold and silver cups that his dad Nebuchadnezzar had stolen from the temple. As a matter of fact, Belshazzar got so intoxicated one time that he started hallucinating and seeing a hand on the wall.

Xerxes shuts the party down and calls for a sorcerer to help him. Xerxes is partying with the noble men of Susa. Vashti is hosting a party for the noble women of Susa. At this time men and women did not party together. Xerxes gets so drunk that he sends for Queen Vashti to come and dance naked for his friends and when she refuses, he is not at all trying to hear that. After all, he is a man of power, a political leader. But her refusal to come and dance before his boys isn't just about him. His boys are extremely concerned about what it will mean for households all over the 127 provinces.

Esther 1:17, 18 lets us know the real reason for concern: "For the queen's conduct will become known to all the women, and so they will despise their husbands and say, 'King Xerxes commanded Queen Vashti to be brought before him, but she would not come. This very day the Persian and Median women of the nobility who have heard about the queen's conduct will respond to all the king's nobles in the same way. There will be no end of disrespect and discord.' "

Those men were scared Vashti would start a revolution! That's why they urge Xerxes to take swift action. He, after consulting with other men, strips her of her title as queen and kicks her out of the palace.

Vashti, because she stands up for herself, has to go through some trials. She has to suffer. She loses her home, her power, influence, and everything else, all because she chooses to take a stand. The fact that she is pretty doesn't save her. I ask myself where are the women who were partying with Vashti in the beginning of chapter 1. They are absent. They say nothing. They do nothing. Vashti stands alone. She does not waver. She is willing to give it all up for her integrity.

But this isn't the message we usually hear when it comes to Vashti's story. Most people who read Esther don't pay attention to Vashti, but of those who do, many just disregard Vashti as a woman who was disobedient. But I see it differently. The story behind the story implies that Vashti was a woman who chose to assert herself and retain her dignity and not dance naked in front of a bunch of men. I don't see her as a villain. I see her as a strong woman. She was not going to let her husband exploit her, showing her off as a trophy. Men like to collect trophies. They collect them in various sizes and shapes. They were doing it then, just as they do it now.

What is a private matter between a husband and a wife becomes a legislative enactment, as the king issues a proclamation that all the women of the land are required by law to respect their husbands.

Some things just don't change. Even today, we see private matters turned into public spectacles meant to put pressure on women. Some religious groups try to legislate what women should wear, for example, proclaiming jewelry, makeup, and certain clothing to be unfit. Yet, there are no such constraints for men. Still others try to put undue pressure on women when it comes to their bodies. Some groups ban contraception, for example, effectively taking choice out of a woman's hands when that is a matter between her and God. Still others try to force women to take certain actions as mothers — actions that should be left up to individual preference, such as to work or not work, breastfeed or not breastfeed. All of these are examples of public, societal pressure put on women when it comes to matters best left up to private choice.

As we continue the story of Vashti, we come to Esther. The king looks among all the pretty, young virgins of the land to find his next wife — the replacement to Vashti. He sees Esther and is smitten with her. He takes her to be his wife. So it's because of what Vashti went through that sets the platform for Esther to be in the palace. Had Vashti not said no and been extricated, there would be no place for Esther. So we as women must understand that there were women who came before to pave the way for us today. There were women who were divorced, put out, demoted, disrespected, just so we could reap the benefits of their sacrifices. I think about my grandmother, Agnes Lewis Wade, who was a presser at a laundry. She spent her life making sacrifices so I could be educated. I think about the women who suffered indignities of civil rights struggles so I could have the opportunity today to go places they only dreamed.

I think about the women who worked countless hours to help me get off drugs, learn to read, and find a new sense of self.

Esther stood on Vashti's shoulders. Whose sacrifices paved the way for you? Whose shoulders do you stand on today? Too often, we don't even pay attention to the women who came before us. We think we are accomplishing things on our own and in a vacuum. I wonder if Esther, with her pretty little self, ever sought out Vashti to just say, "Thank you, sister," or if she just enjoyed the benefits of the palace with no regard to what came before?

The story of Esther does not end with Esther assuming the role of queen. Esther is elevated out of nowhere and placed in a high position. At first glance it may appear to you that she rises to this position because she is beautiful, but she rises to this position because God has a plan. Her rise has a purpose.

One of the king's men wants to have the Jews killed. He cons the king into letting him issue an order for that very act. Mordecai, who raised Esther and is responsible for her coming to the attention of the king, tells Esther that she must do something. Dressed like a bum in sackcloth, Mordecai goes to the palace.

"Do not think that because you are in the king's house you alone of all the Jews will escape. For if you remain silent at this time, relief and deliverance for the Jews will arise from another place, but you and your family will perish. And who knows but that you have come to royal position for such a time as this?" Mordecai says in Esther 4:13, 14.

Esther knows she has to do something. She calls her handmaidens — her girls — to fasting and praying, and tells the rest of the Jews to do the same thing. The revolution that Vashti started continues. As Esther calls the sorority together to fast and pray, the Lord begins to reveal a strategy. Esther begins to take the king back to what he is familiar with. She invites him to a banquet, along with Haman, the guy who has schemed to have the Jews killed. They go through a series of banquets and the king ends up asking her what she wants. Esther, who has the king's favor, asks the king to save her people.

The king does, and orders that Haman — the one who issued the order to have the Jews killed — be killed instead.

In the beginning of the story, the king starts out demanding that Vashti come out to dance naked. But by the end of the story, he is begging Esther to tell him what she wants. Good looks weren't enough, but fasting and praying were. So no matter where we are, if we are in the palace or the valley, we have to be able to hear from God.

The story behind the story reveals that there is a seed

God has placed on the inside of every woman that He wants to give birth. He wants to give birth to purpose through us. In Esther's case, that purpose had a huge impact, as for generations and generations, a nation was saved, as a result of one woman standing on the shoulders of another woman who connected with a group of other women who happened to be her employees. Esther was in the palace. The other women were her handmaids. They were strategically placed. Even today, a lot of us are strategically placed. We are CEOs. We are at the top of Fortune 500 companies. We are lawmakers. We are activists. We are among the elite in our fields. We aren't there just for show. We are there to do a work. We can create change because of our positions. We can help to enact laws, change policy, and create organizations.

We can't waste those opportunities.

We must be utilitarian in our approach to ministry to women. Like Esther, who rises to prominence on the shoulders of another woman and uses her position for the greater good of society, so must we.

Sisters, we have been given great gifts, benefits, and blessings. We cannot sit on them and use them only for our selfish needs. This work that God has for us is much bigger than that. Instead, we must use our gifts, talents, and blessings to touch lives. Esther's story illustrates this fact. When we stand on the shoulders of others who have sacrificed for us, we owe it to them and to God to do something with that sacrifice.

There is not a sister reading this who does not have a talent, skill, or gift. God does not create us without giving us something to offer. So use your blessing to be a blessing to another sister. Then go beyond her and be a blessing to others. What gift, skill, or talent do you possess?

Do you sing? Do you write? Do you have an eye for design? Are you super organized? Can you break down complex matters into bits of information others can understand? Do you find that you get along with everybody? Do you have a way with numbers? Do you see life from a different perspective? Are you able to relate to others? Each of these questions points to a talent, gift, or skill.

If you know what your talent, gift, or skill is, that is wonderful. Go forth now and share it! But if you are like many sisters and you are not sure, then your assignment right now is to pray and think about it until you discover what it is. Then use it to enhance life for others.

This isn't just me speaking. This is a message from God. He has placed you here with purpose, as we have discussed, and He has given you abilities to fulfill that purpose. Your current circumstances are not an excuse for not using your talents, skills, or abilities.

So you've dropped out of school and you know you need to get back? Well, that's not a reason to refuse to use your gift. So you're in a marriage that is suffocating you? Again, not a reason to refuse to use your gift. So you are swamped at work? Nope. Not a reason to refuse to use your gift.

Many times we say we will use our gifts, walk in purpose, or do big, meaningful actions once everything is just so. Once all the ducks are in a row, that's when we will step out on faith and do the thing God has called us to do. Well, sisters, I'm here to say that things will never be perfect. So you've just got to work with what you have right now.

If you go back and read the fourth chapter of Esther, you will see that Esther had to be pushed to take action. Mordecai gave her a reality check. She had been an orphan girl and he raised her. And so he told her she had a responsibility. That's why she had been placed in this palace position anyway. He had to nudge her along.

So if you have to be pushed to take action, if you have to be nudged along, consider this that push or nudge.

God allows us to come to those points in life where we have a reality check. He reminds us of where we're from and that he brought us through. Although we may be teaching at the university now, we are the same child that struggled to read in third grade. We may live in the suburbs today, but we remember living in the projects with black and white TV not too long ago. So Mordecai reminded her she wasn't always in the palace and that she was set up by God to be part of His plan.

Mordecai wrapped up by telling her if she remains silent,

God would use someone else. The same applies today. If you don't want to teach Sunday school, if you don't want to work in the teen ministry with pregnant girls, if you don't want to sing in the choir, someone else will. God always has a spare tire. But you will never be fulfilled until you do what God has created you to do.

Abigail: Married to a fool

1 Samuel 25

The young David is on the run in the wilderness from King Saul. He and his men need some money, or at least food, so he offers protection to a wealthy sheep shearer, Nabal. Nabal thumbs his nose at David and pretty much treats him like nothing, even though David's protection saves Nabal's sheep.

When David finds out about Nabal's response, he becomes angry and swears that he will kill Nabal and every male of his household. David takes 400 of his 600 men and heads to find Nabal.

But Nabal's servants rush back to tell Abigail, Nabal's wife, of her husband's misconduct. The servants let her know Nabal insulted David and his men, who had been kind to them and even looked out for their sheep while camped nearby.

Abigail, a beautiful and quick-thinking woman, immediately goes into action. She gathers large amounts of food, some servants, and hops on a donkey to go find David, unbeknownst to her husband.

When she finds David, she apologizes for her husband and offers the food she has prepared. She asks that David spare her family and to let bygones be bygones.

David, no doubt impressed by her beauty and the food, agrees. He calls off his men and they do not harm Nabal. Abigail goes back home to find her husband in a drunken party, celebrating his wealth.

She doesn't say anything to him that night about the situation, but waits until he is sober in the morning, then tells him what she did. He has a heart attack and is paralyzed before dying a week later. No doubt, the shock of his wife's quick thinking was too much for him.

David sends for Abigail and marries her.

***

This story behind the story is full of so many good tidbits of information! It's immediately something we can relate to, even thousands of years later. What's the first thing that struck you about this story? Probably the fact that Abigail was married to a fool! And that's not my word, that's the Bible's.

Check out 1 Samuel 25:25: "Please pay no attention, my lord, to that wicked man Nabal. He is just like his name — his name means Fool, and folly goes with him ... ."

Abigail knows her husband is foolish and she probably isn't surprised to hear of the incident with David and his men. Seems that beautiful and smart women were marrying fools back then and unfortunately, we're still doing it today.

I can't tell you how many times I've counseled women who are in the same position. They are with men who make ill-advised decisions, don't listen, and cause a bunch of ruckus. If you are a woman who is married to a man who makes poor choices, you know the disastrous results that can happen. The man's poor choices can result in loss of job, income, business, home, health, even life!

Abigail's example helps us figure out how to deal with that situation. I believe God included her story in His Word as a way to counsel us women on how to make good choices, even when those around us make poor decisions. Abigail kept a cool head and was swift to action. She knew she couldn't turn a blind eye to her husband's misdeeds. The same goes for us today. When our mates commit grave offenses that affect our families in a negative way, we can't sit back and let whatever happens, happen.

Like Abigail, we can use wisdom and good judgment to figure out a positive solution.

There is another point here that I don't want you to miss. Abigail didn't go running to her husband to fuss and fight before making her move. She probably knew that if she confronted Nabal about his actions, all he would do would be to argue with her. He'd just try to go around in circles in a negative conversation that would produce nothing.

So she didn't even go there. She just did what she needed to do.

This isn't to say you should just make decisions and never discuss them with your husband. I wouldn't suggest that. A man and wife should be on one accord. But when you know your man is not capable of making the right decision and confronting him about his bad decision will only create drama, sometimes the best thing to do is to handle the situation and then talk to him about it later.

Another thing Abigail did is that she waited until Nabal was sober before discussing the matter. Sometimes we must wait for the right moment before we break something to our men or try to have serious discussions. If you know your man is stressed out when he comes home from work, that's probably not the right time to tell him that Johnny got a D in math. Wait a little while. Give him time to take off his work clothes or to relax a bit. If you know your man is already ticked off about the fact that his brother wrecked his car, that's probably not the time to tell him the insurance just went up. Timing can make a huge difference in the outcome of your discussion.

Abigail's story ends with her transitioning from being married to a fool to being married to a king. How do you go from being married to a fool to being married to a king, sisters? There is no training in between. I am certain that Abigail had some baggage that David was forced to deal with. She probably had some baggage in the front closet and some baggage outside in the shed. The baggage in the front closet came up often and every now and then she brought out the baggage from the shed. Many of us have been married to Nabal. How will we respond to David in the next season of life?

Tamar: Rape survivor

2 Samuel 13

Tamar is raped by her brother Amnon, who schemes to get

her alone with him. Amnon, who lusts after her, even though she is his sister, pretends to be sick so she will come and take care of him and fix him some food. She does, and that's when he attacks her.

Tamar begs him not to do this because she, like he, knows it is wrong. But he doesn't listen. Once he finishes brutalizing Tamar, his infatuation turns to disgust and he casts her from his home. She cries bitterly, as the pain of what happened sets in. Her brother Absalom asks her if Amnon has forced himself on her and she says yes.

Absalom tells her to be quiet and not to take it to heart. Tamar, now desolate, goes to live with Absalom. After a while, Absalom kills Amnon.

Tamar's story touches many women because so many have been raped, one way or the other. Most women have been raped mentally and emotionally. That's why we do not trust our men to lead us or trust them to provide for and take care of us. And as a result of us being raped physically and mentally, we have been rejected over and over again. Like Tamar, we have become desolate and heartbroken.

It's interesting that Amnon claims to have loved Tamar so much, but as soon as he has his way with her, he casts her out, telling her he hates her. I believe that is because she knew his secret; she knew what kind of man he really was.

A lot of times we come into the lives of our men and God exposes their secrets or sin to us and, as with Amnon, they begin to hate us because we know. That hatred only grows. We end up even more hurt.

A lot of our men reprimand us by running to other women. That makes us feel even more shameful and guilty. That threatens all of our emotional security, financial security, and sexual security. It is painful. At the end of the day, we have a heavy burden.

What's worse is that we aren't even given permission to express our feelings. In Tamar's case, Absalom told her basically to just chill out. Don't take it to heart, is what he told her. Don't say anything. That's the state of literally millions of women, especially Black women. We have taken it. We have held it in. We mask it in education, in jobs. On the inside we've internalized it. We become infected. That infection is a fever that breaks out into a cancer. That cancer spreads across our psyche, cannibalizing everything in its path. The result is we become only shells of the vibrant, engaging women we once were.

Something on the inside keeps us feeling low self-esteem, feeling all alone. It infects us to the extent that it even infects our wombs. So now when we give birth to little boys and little girls, it already infects them. We pass on low self-esteem and poor self-worth to our children.

We shut our mouths and never tell how we were mentally or physically raped or molested.

Let's break free from the curse that followed Tamar. It is time to speak out. We don't have to be quiet or "just deal with it," if someone wrongs us in such a horrendous way. We have a right to speak about it, to seek help, to seek justice.

Tamar is the woman inside each of us who has been wronged in this way. She is crying out and saying to every man, "Hear my cry. I come with some baggage."

She is saying: "Hear my cry. That's why I have to check your cell phone. That's why I don't trust you."

She is saying: "Hear my cry. I can't help but be strong and independent. I can't help but stand on the fact that I have made my own money. I've been hurt and now I know I need to protect myself. I have no one to depend on. I can't let my guard down. I want to, but I don't know what to do about the pain I'm in."

Men need to hear our cry. We've been quiet long enough.

The story behind the story tells us that Tamar's cry isn't just about the hurt she has experienced. She also represents the women who do want to lean on their men, who do want to find refuge there. Women, we have been very ineffective in expressing our hurt. We must let these men know that we need them to take their rightful place as the leader in the home, community, and church. We need our man to know we need him to be our lover, not our daddy. "I need you to be the man God has created and designed you to be," we need to say. "Yeah, I have been getting by raising my children and doing things on my own. But I need you."

Sisters, I know our pain makes these words nearly impossible to speak, but speak them, we must. If we don't let our men know we want them around — that we need them — then another generation of real love will be lost. Let them know so they can be a part of our healing.

Bringing Tamar's story back around to women reaching women, it's interesting to me that no other woman is mentioned in her story. And I know there were some women around! But where were they? Where were her sisters? Where were her girlfriends? Who embraced her when she emerged from Amnon's house, bruised and broken?

I know it's a touchy subject, but I must address it. Too many times we as women turn a blind eye to another's hurt. Mothers suspect daddies or uncles are molesting their children, but they ignore the signs. They don't want to "rock the boat," or cause drama. Yet, they allow their children to be unprotected, in their very homes. If that's not some drama, I don't know what is. Other times, we as women act as if we don't see the obvious signs of hurt or abuse on others around us. We prefer to pretend all is well because we don't want to get involved.

That is unacceptable. How can we leave our sisters to hurt alone?

Tamar must have felt so small as she realized the women around her didn't think enough of her to reach out a hand. Are we afraid hurt or pain will rub off on us? Is that why we don't want to reach out to each other more often?

You know I am passionate about women reaching women. That is the theme of this entire book. I feel so strongly about it because I know just what a difference it can make. I know this from my own life experience. When I was in the hospital sick with cancer, women were the ones who ministered to me. They were the ones who fed me when I couldn't feed myself. God birthed the whole Dr. Rosalind Osgood Ministries International concept at that time. Women were the ones who were there when my second husband — someone I had been with for eighteen years — divorced me while I was battling cancer. When I was on chemo and my grandmother — Mama — was ill and I couldn't go, they would go sit with her. Those women helped me through my most different times. God showed me how important it is for women to help other women.

If you're a sister who is a bit out of practice when it comes to reaching out to other women, here is an exercise you can try. The next time you come across a woman in need, just pause for a moment. I'm not asking you to do anything at all. Just pause. Too often in our rush-rush lives, we zip from one activity to the other, never taking the time to even consider our actions. We never give ourselves a chance to respond to anything a little outside of our focus. So in this exercise, start with pausing.

Maybe you'll encounter the sister on the elevator as you two arrive at the office. Maybe you'll encounter her at church as you two make your exit. Maybe you'll bump into her in the airport, the grocery store, or at your child's school. There will be something about her that will let you know she needs you. Maybe it will be the look in her eyes. Maybe it will be the conversation you overhear as she gets off her cell. Maybe it will be the tone of her voice.

Whatever it is, when you pause, that will give you an opportunity to assess the situation and consider reaching out to her.

When you pause, ask yourself: "What is the best thing I can do in this situation?" Then answer it. Maybe the sister just needs a smile. Maybe she needs to hear a scripture that has been on your heart. Maybe she needs you to share with her a similar story from you about how you dealt with a particular situation. Your answer will come based on what you assess as the needs of the situation, the forum, and appropriate action. Of course, whether the sister is someone you know or someone you've just met will determine too, how you respond. But don't let the fact that she is a stranger put you off, for we are all women and in that, sisters. So while we may be new to each other, we are still family.

After you've paused for that moment and asked yourself that question, respond appropriately. Even if it's only a smile, sometimes that smile can be the difference in someone's day. I've found myself literally at my wits' end, only to look up and receive a smile or kind word from someone and that gave me new energy to keep going on. So a smile can make a tremendous difference. Imagine what a hug, genuine offer of help, or encouragement can do.

I am very intentional about reaching out to other women. I go out of my way to interact with other women. For example, if I am in a conference or workshop setting I have a rule: I exchange contact information with at least three women before leaving, and I make sure to follow up within 48 hours.

Ruth And Naomi: The bond of widows

Book of Ruth

Ruth's story is one of survival, loyalty, and success. Elimelech, Naomi's husband, takes her and they leave Bethlehem where there is a famine and go to live in the country of Moab. It is like going from a nice place to a garbage dump. But Naomi goes.

Elimelech is seeking prosperity. His faith is not strong enough to stay in Bethlehem where there is a famine. With his natural eyes Moab looks a lot better. But the Moabites live a sinful lifestyle. They worship idols, sacrifice their children to those idols, and perform all manner of other acts foreign to the Israelites.

After a while, Naomi's husband dies and she is left with her two sons, Mahlon and Chilion, whose names mean sickly and failing, respectively. Her boys, after living in this place, find and marry Moabite women, Orpah and Ruth. After about ten years, they too die. So now Naomi is left with her daughters-in-law in a strange land.

Naomi's emotions make her bitter. She has lost everything. She has no man, no money, no mansion, and no means of making it on her own. In ancient Hebrew times women depended on their husbands for survival. And with her sons gone, she feels that God has turned His back on her.

She decides it's time to go back home to the familiar. She has heard the famine is over so she's ready to ditch Moab and get back to what she knows. She tells her daughters-in-law to return to their mothers' houses.

Ruth 1:8-13 outlines what happened: "Then Naomi said to her two daughters-in-law, 'Go back, each of you, to your mother's home. May the Lord show you kindness, as you have shown kindness to your dead husbands and to me. May the Lord grant that each of you will find rest in the home of another husband.

"Then she kissed them goodbye and they wept aloud and said to her, 'We will go back with you to your people.'" "But Naomi said, 'Return home, my daughters. Why would you come with me? Am I going to have any more sons, who could become your husbands? Return home, my daughters; I am too old to have another husband. Even if I thought there was still hope for me — even if I had a husband tonight and then gave birth to sons — would you wait until they grew up? Would you remain unmarried for them? No, my daughters. It is more bitter for me than for you, because the Lord's hand has turned against me!'"

Orpah agrees and returns to Moab. Ruth, though, remains steadfast.

She begs to go with Naomi.

See it in Ruth 1:16,17: "But Ruth replied, 'Don't urge me to leave you or to turn back from you. Where you go I will go, and where you stay I will stay. Your people will be my people and your God my God. Where you die I will die, and there I will be buried. May the Lord deal with me, be it ever so severely, if even death separates you and me.'"

So Naomi and Ruth head to Bethlehem. Everyone is excited to see Naomi and they call out to her. But she is so bitter she tells them not to call her by that name anymore and to instead call her Mara, because God has made her life bitter.

Naomi and Ruth settle in Bethlehem. Ruth decides to go and try to make a way for them, after all, they've got to eat. It is harvest time, so she goes out and follows the harvesters, picking up the dropped and discarded pieces of barley.

She happens to be following harvEsthers working the fields of Boaz, a relative of Naomi's husband. Boaz notices Ruth and inquires about her. Someone gives him the rundown and he tells his people not to harm her and to make sure they drop plenty of barley for her to gather.

He pulls Ruth to the side and tells her she doesn't need to go anywhere else. She can pick up barley on his land. She is immediately touched and grateful and asks how she gained such favor. He tells her he has heard how kind she has been to her mother-in-law.

Boaz ends up marrying Ruth. Ruth has a son, whom Naomi gets to care for as a grandmother. Ruth's son is the grandfather of King David.

***

The story of Ruth and Naomi is so good! It has so many elements to it. On the one hand, it is about loyalty, because Ruth showed a fierce loyalty and love for her mother-in-law, choosing to go with and look after her instead of going back to her own people.

On the other hand, it is a story of redemption. Naomi feels bitterness at having lost so much. But God gives her a new life through Ruth, who gets married again and has a son that Naomi gets to look after and love.

The story also makes another point, sisters. It doesn't matter where you've come from in life. God can still use you to do great and mighty work. Ruth came from a land of wicked practices, idol worship, incest, and all manner of evil. But she didn't let her background keep her from the future God had for her. She was humble and kind, and let her character speak for her, instead. And God chose to bless her abundantly. In my spiritual imagination, I know her life was better with Boaz than it ever was with Naomi's son. Boaz was wealthy, healthy, and kind. And, they had a son together.

What this means for us today is that, as has been said elsewhere in this book, your background does not have to define you. We all have a past, and sometimes our pasts can be pretty bad. But by God's grace, we can overcome the past and go forward and do great and mighty things. Ruth overcame her past and became the great-grandmother of a mighty king. What's more, through her lineage, Jesus was born.

Now, that's something!

Jesus, the son of God, chose to come through the line

of a Moabite woman whose people worshipped idols. In contemporary language,

Ruth was a little nappy-headed girl, from the wrong family and the wrong town. She ended up marrying the right man and being in the lineage of Jesus.

As we talk about Ruth and the beautiful thing she did, I also want to take a moment to address Naomi. Naomi was broken. She blamed God for her misfortune. Naomi's worldview was that God is sovereign. God knows all. God sees all. God is responsible for everything, both good and bad. She responded by saying "El Shaddai or Almighty God has dealt bitterly with me." In God's permissive will He had allowed these things to happen to Naomi.

As my father in the ministry, Dr. Mack King Carter, says in his book "Interpreting the Will of God," "God, in His permissive will, permits some things to happen to us." God is a master teacher. He gives us tests to strengthen our faith. James also reminds us that we are tempted by our own fleshly desires and when we fall to temptation we have to pay the consequences.

So even if God allows something unfortunate to happen to us, that does not diminish who God is. When something great happens to us, we often like to say, "God is so good!" We celebrate God all day then. But what about when something bad happens? We don't proclaim His goodness then. But I am here to say God is good all the time. And God is God. So whether you are feeling blessed or whether you are feeling bitter, God is the same God. We can't bless His name only when the good happens and turn bitter as soon as something bad comes.

Often, the bad thing turns out to help us later on. Consider Naomi's situation. Her husband and sons died, which was bad, but that sequence of events got her back to her homeland of Bethlehem, away from the idol worship. I can't help but think getting away from those pagan traditions had to be a good thing. And from the deal, she ultimately got a child who was like a grandson to her.

Naomi could not immediately see her blessings, of course. That's why she was bitter. But don't turn your nose up at her. We are guilty of the same thing. Sometimes we are so caught up in our emotions that we can't see the blessings of

God. We are too busy whining and feeling sorry for ourselves. As Christians who say we are on the battlefield we spend too much time placating Satan instead of pleasing God.

As Naomi looks at her life, she laments in Ruth 1:21: "I went away full, but the Lord has brought me back empty."

She was bankrupt inside and outside.

Have you ever been in that place? Maybe it was when after being married 20 years, your spouse came in and told you he wanted a divorce. Or your good child called you from jail because he or she had committed some awful crime. At times like these it appears that all of your praying and all your parenting appears to have been in vain. Perhaps you made some decisions that caused you to lose everything inwardly and outwardly. Perhaps you chose to just take one drink and that one drink 10 years later landed you homeless in jail in a state of incomprehensible demoralization.

Naomi came to understand that only through emptiness could she enjoy God's blessing in the fields of barley harvest. The emptiness in her soul was going to be the way to a greater discovery and experience of God's blessing and nearness. In order for us to enjoy the blessings of God through other women, we need to be emptied of self. We must be emptied of all of our natural, fleshly self-importance and selfishness. The Bible tells us that we must die to self.

Emotional bankruptcy will either make us or break us. There have been times when my life has been flooded with headaches, heartbreak, and the feeling of helplessness. The enemy was busy trying to convince me he had won. He wanted me to believe that God had taken His hands off me. He attacked my mind. His ultimate goal was to make me believe that God had taken His anointing from me and that God had taken his spirit from within me. Allow me to use this analogy. There have been times that I have found myself on a dead-end street. I didn't know which way to go or where to turn. I felt like I was fenced in and my enemies had me surrounded. I was just about to give up or surrender to the enemy but God showed up and gave me a detour sign that led me back to the main highway so that I could get back into His plan and purpose for my life. What is so challenging is the fact that sometimes before I can get back on the main highway I have to pay a toll. I would prefer not to pay the toll. I believe that God includes the toll so that once I am back on the main highway I will be more attentive to His voice and less likely to get off on the wrong exit again. The toll is the pain or the price I have to pay for residing in dead-end places. That's the case for each of us. God's desire is to have a perpetual presence in our lives.

Although I have to pay the toll, God is with me. He pleads my case through the eyes of mercy. I left home in the fall of 1983 to attend college at Florida A & M University. I was young, athletic, and destined for success. The fall of 1987 I returned home. I was now a college drop-out, pregnant out of wedlock, and battling addiction. Like Naomi, I left home full and came back empty. I am so glad God specializes in making miracles out of my mess. I have been in many dark places but God has redeemed me and helped me find the light over and over again.

The story of Ruth has one other element I want to bring out. It goes to the theme of this book: women helping women. Ruth and Naomi helped each other. We often hear about mothers-in-law and daughters-in-law at odds. Popular culture tells us these women just can't get along. Ruth and Naomi's story paints a different picture. Not only did they get along, but they held a deep love.

Ruth could have gone back to her family and Naomi would have had no hard feelings. Instead, Ruth stayed with the old woman, knowing Naomi had no one and nothing else.

God blessed Naomi through a young Moabite woman. This young girl gave up everything. Ruth says, "If you are poor, I will be poor with you. I am willing to give up my hometown. I am willing to leave my stomping ground where everybody knows my name."

Ruth says, "I am even willing to give up big mamma's house to follow this old woman to Bethlehem."

The story behind the story features this young Moabite girl who takes a risk and makes an investment in a friendship. Naomi arrives back in Bethlehem, bitter and broken but not alone. When the whole town is gossiping about her she has a friend by the name of Ruth who stands with her.

Ruth was willing to sacrifice herself for her mother-in-law. She was willing to reach out to this woman.

In turn, Naomi helped Ruth by mentoring her. She told her what to do to get Boaz to marry her and she helped Ruth learn new customers in her new land. And Ruth helped Naomi even more. She gave Naomi a new chance at life. She made sure Naomi was fed and even gave Naomi a child that was like a grandson to her. Chapter four says Naomi was restored. She had hope again. She could smile again. She could live again.

Ruth, I believe, saved Naomi's life.

Rahab: A woman with a divine destiny

Joshua 1 and 2

The Israelites wandered in the wilderness from 1446-1406 — 40 years. Around 1405 B.C., Joshua succeeded Moses and in chapter one we see that Joshua makes preparations to cross the Jordan and possess the land the Lord promised the Israelites through Moses. Chapter two begins with the Israelites in the Acacia Grove. The Acacia Grove is the Hebrew word Shittim, which means Acacia trees.

This is another name for a staging area of Israel, across the Jordan from Jericho.

About three days before they are to cross the Jordan River, Joshua sends two messengers to Jericho to spy on the land. Joshua wants the spies to bring him information of Jericho's walls and gates, and its state of preparation. During this time there is not centralized government in Canaan.

Instead, each city runs its own affairs. If Joshua can conquer Jericho he can split the Canaanite army. His strategy is to divide and conquer. He will attack the weak forces in the south first then deal with the stronger forces in the north. Jericho is also a good place to set up camp because it is well supplied with water and food. It is an oasis for a campsite about 5 miles from the Jordan River.

The spies arrive in Jericho at the house of Rahab, the harlot of Jericho. How could these two spies end up in the house of this prostitute? Oh look at God. We never know who God is going to use to help us.

Rahab, the Canaanite prostitute of Jericho, is a woman of divine destiny. She is a woman who has been deliberately chosen. Hand picked by God. God has branded her for this particular assignment.

Let's look at Rahab, up close. Rahab belongs to an idolatrous people, and has a name meaning broad, spaciousness, or fierceness. Some scholars have tried to clean Rahab up and suggest that she was an innkeeper. Others say she had been reduced to prostitution because of the death of her husband and by the needs of her impoverished family. But the Bible clearly identifies her as a harlot.

A woman with a divine destiny might be a woman who comes from a dysfunctional family background. Rahab, the daughter of the Gentiles, descends from a race doomed to destruction. Rahab's parents are of the condemned race of the Canaanites. Her parents have no faith in God, themselves. Rahab is not in a believing country. In the entire city of Jericho it appears that she is the only believer in her family initially. Behavioral psychologists always talk about the influence family culture and behaviors have on the individual. We can look at our families and see many similarities, but I believe we also see differences.

A woman with a divine destiny might be a woman who is branded by her past. Rahab is a prostitute. Her profession is lucrative but it is not amiable. She has profitable relationships with men. You know all the sisters hate her, because if the truth were to be told, every man who goes to town wants to go to Rahab's house. She is a well-known prostitute.

This woman is plagued by her past. She is stigmatized. I find it interesting that our pre-salvific days follow us forever. I am perplexed at how God can change my name. Take me from being a drunk to being a preacher, from being a meaningless mess of a woman to being a miracle. Take me from being a dirty, filthy wrench to being His amazing grace. Take me from being helpless, homeless, and hopeless, to being saved, sanctified, and suited for a seat in Glory. But some folk will continue to focus on my deficits. What I used to be.

Let me minister to your heart right now. We all keep struggling with some stuff. We have various thorns in our flesh. You might have been praying and begging God to remove yours. God allowed me to write this book to tell you that He is working it out for your good. He might not remove it. In 2 Corinthians 12:7 Paul says: "Therefore, in order to keep me from becoming conceited, I was given a thorn in my flesh, a messenger of Satan, to torment me."

The word given is in the passive voice meaning that there is an outside entity doing something to the subject. Paul says a thorn, thalaps in the Greek — an irritating thing in my flesh (Soax) — is to buffet me. In the Greek the word Paul uses for buffet means to slap or hit. It is in the present tense so it means it is happening now.

This problem that you have, God in His permissive will, allows it to remain present so you can pray. Paul prayed three times and God responded by saying my grace is sufficient. God's grace is sufficient. He is helping you not to be a glory grabber.

That thorn keeps you in touch with who God is. It keeps you humble. It helps you not believe your own propaganda.

My Master's grace is sufficient. He gives it to us in the right measure. He gives it to me in abundance. God keeps delivering me from the dark caves of life. He has spared me for this assignment. He spared Rahab for her assignment. And maybe he's preparing you for yours right now.

A woman with a divine destiny is a woman who exhibits her faith by taking a risk. She is not afraid. Rahab literally puts her life on the line to hide these spies. She commits treason against her own people. What Rahab has heard about God empowers her to turn away from the evil and corrupt ways of the Canaanites. In other words, she exhibits her faith by repenting.

In Joshua 2:9, Rahab expresses her faith by using God's personal name Yahweh, translated here as Lord, indicating that she has come to have faith in the living God. God has divinely opened the heart and mind of a foreign prostitute to accept Him as Lord. Rahab says, "I know that the Lord has given you this land and that a great fear of you has fallen on us, so that all who live in this country are melting in fear because of you."

She goes on to articulate two miraculous deliverances. She speaks of the Red Sea and the victory over two Amorite kings east of the Jordan. She has never gone to a worship service. She is not a frequenter in any ecclesiastical setting. Yet, she has heard about God and what He has done for the Israelites and she believes. In verse 11c she says, "For the Lord your God is God in heaven above and on the earth below."

Rahab has a strong conviction about God. Her conviction about God makes her concerned about the salvation of others. In verses 12 and 13, she negotiates with the spies to ensure that her family will be saved from destruction.

***

As her story continues we are told in verse 15 that Rahab let the men down the wall by a cord through the window that led them to safety. The cord was made of flax and dyed red, from the cochineal grub, which produces a scarlet or purple dye. Isaiah 1:18 says, "Though your sins be as scarlet, they shall be as white as snow. Though they are red like crimson, they shall be as wool."

As once an immoral woman, her sins are scarlet. So are ours. Her hope of cleansing was as real as ours, for our sure hope is in the Lord Jesus' death. The rope carried the weight of each man as they slithered down the flax cord. Jesus carries our weight. In 1 Peter 2:24, we find that by our Lord's stripes, we are healed.

Sisters, Isaiah 53:5 is still good: "But He was pierced for our transgressions, he was crushed for our iniquities; the punishment that brought us peace was on him, and by his wounds we are healed."

Oh, the power of the blood of God's Lamb! A woman of divine destiny is covered by the blood of Jesus the Christ. In the words of a favorite hymn, His blood reaches to the highest mountain. His blood reaches to the lowest valley. It is His blood that gives me strength from day to day. I am so glad that His blood will never lose its power.

The story behind the story makes it clear that a woman of divine destiny finishes well. Rahab eventually marries

Salmon, one of the two spies she sheltered. Salmon is a prince of the house of Judah. Let me make it plain: This heathen prostitute marries into one of the leading families of Israel. She becomes the mother of Boaz, who marries Ruth. Their son is Obed, the father of Jesse. Jesse is David's father. Jesus comes through this line generations later. In other words, Rahab becomes the grandmother of Boaz, who marries Ruth, and then the great, great, grandmother of David — the mighty king of Israel. Our Lord Jesus was a natural descendant of this Canaanite prostitute from Jericho. This woman of divine destiny whom the Hebrew writer listed in the hall a fame of faith lived a purpose beyond her past.

Sister, you may start out wrong. You may have you back against the wall. It may be the fourth quarter and you might have three minutes left in the game and you are down by 10 points. The enemy has already rendered you defeated. Satan has started a cosmic blog. The entries read: "She is too depressed to win." "She is too abused." "Her self-esteem is depleted." "She has been raped and exploited; she can never amount to anything." "She has messed up too many times." "She is a perpetual failure."

But I am blogging back on your behalf today. I want to post on the walls of your mind that Jesus is the ultimate go-to player. No matter how far down you are, He can bring you back. He is the kind of God who can reach way, way down and pick you up. I am a Baptist preacher, and I feel my help coming on right here. I am so glad that over 2000 years ago Jesus looked down the corridors of time and knew that on December 2, 1989, I would be sitting in a Volusia county jail — desolated, discombobulated and in a state of incomprehensive demoralization. He knew that I would begin to call on His name. He rescued me from the hands of the enemy. The enemy keeps trying to kill me. But I am a woman of divine destiny, and so are you. God has great plans for your life. You have been predestined for a divine destiny. Stop looking back. Stop being like Lot's wife. She could not move on from the past. She became a monument. You have been sitting still for too long. You are a woman of divine destiny. God didn't bring you through all that you've gone through for you to be a monument. You must be a movement. Keep it moving my sister. God wants to use your past to bring glory to Himself in your future.

WOMEN REACHING WOMEN MOMENT

Think of at least two women in your life who can benefit from hearing about at least one of the Biblical stories of women you've just read. What is going on in their lives that makes these stories relevant to them? Consider reaching out to them to share these stories and encourage them as they face their challenges. Women must be intentional about reaching other women.

"Jesus answered: It is written: 'Man shall not live on bread alone, but on every word that comes from the mouth of God.'" – Matthew 4:4

4 Sisterly Bonds Develop Through Experiences

Whereas I was kicking the drug habit and getting my life back on track, I met a woman who was going through her own drama. We were able to help each other and, 20 years later, we remain best friends.

We were both on house arrest.

"I went to report and didn't see her," my friend Jackie recalls. "I had just met her and now she wasn't there. I had found somebody I wanted to get close to and she was gone."

But our paths crossed again.

"I went to an N.A. meeting one Saturday morning," Jackie recalls. "I saw her come in with three babies. She had one on each side of her and one on her hip."

Jackie asked me where I had been, and I told her I was off house arrest. We exchanged numbers.

She went to a recovery meeting one day, angry with her sponsor who had broken her confidence and shared some of Jackie's private information with her husband who told Jackie's boyfriend. She asked me to be her sponsor instead. At the same time Jackie's health took a turn for the worst.

We decided to begin praying together. Today over two decades later we are still praying Monday through Friday mornings. We have added Paula, Brenda, Connie, and Linda to the group.

"I never thought that one day she would become a pastor," Jackie says of me today. "I stuck by her and went through so many things with her. She would go to work doing two and three jobs. She got her bachelors, her masters, her doctoral degree. I was there to cheer her on. I was there to babysit three kids for her."

Jackie kept my children at night many times while I completed my studies. She and my daughter would sleep in her bed; my sons would sleep on a pallet on the floor. She made sure they had meals. She did whatever she could to help ease my burden as I pursued my education. She wouldn't even accept payment from me. All she wanted to do was to be my friend, my support. My children call her Auntie Jackie.

"Us being recovering alcoholics and addicts, from where we come from, I was proud to see a young lady strive to do better," Jackie says.

We each have come a long way since those days. I've gotten my education and am doing work I love. Jackie has gotten married — even though she has been HIV positive for more than 20 years — and she has bought a home and done many other things. We were there for each other through all of the struggles and all of the blessings.

Jackie was one of those women helping me through my cancer. "Even when she couldn't lift a hand and was barely able to put one foot in front of the other, I was there," she remembers. "I was there when she got out of the hospital and had to leave home the next day because of a marital dispute."

Seeing each other through so many good and bad times created a bond between Jackie and me that life can never erase. That is the power of sisterhood. It doesn't matter that we are not biological sisters. It doesn't matter that we were not raised together. It does not matter that we did not know each other as children. All that matters is that we have created sisterhood through our shared experiences.

We women go through so many of the same things. I may be a mother in Florida with three children in college, but I can still relate to a mother in Kansas raising children herself. Our circumstances may be different, but some of our experiences are the same. These are the things that create bonds.

There are some things that only another woman can relate to; That's why it's so imperative that we reach out to each other. We are here to support and encourage each other. When one of us is down, the other can lift her up. When one of us is going through a tough time, the other can remind her that it will be all right.

"We are here to encourage each one that we can do anything through Jesus Christ," Jackie loves to say. She celebrates women's accomplishments. "To me, it's so important to see women prosper. I'm always here to help another woman and to encourage her."

Jackie tells the story of being in her garage one day when a young woman walked up to her. The young woman asked her, "Ma'am, do you have anything you can give me? I just got an apartment, and I don't have anything."

Jackie's heart went out to the girl. She gave the girl three bags of items for her apartment, many of them wedding gifts she had received when she got married. "I know what it's like just starting out," Jackie says.

The girl shared with Jackie that she was HIV positive. Jackie could relate.

"I contracted HIV when I was on drugs and alcohol," she says. "I was a crack smoker. When I found out I was HIV positive, I thought it was the end of the road. I cried for three hours."

Jackie met a young woman who had been HIV positive for 21 years and that helped her see the disease did not have to be a death sentence. She also met another woman who affirmed her value. "She told me I was worthy and beautiful," Jackie recalls. "That gave me a lot of hope and strength."

Like me, women helped feed her soul and give her the courage to go on.

Jackie feared she would never do many of the things we consider normal, such as have another boyfriend or get married. Her boyfriend ended up becoming her husband! He accepted her and they went on to build a life together. Twenty years later, they are still together.

Jackie recalls seeing Magic Johnson go public with the news that he had HIV. She marveled that if he could go public, so could she. I knew how Magic's story encouraged her and I knew many others needed to hear it, so I invited him to speak at our church. Jackie felt their stories were similar; except Magic was already married when he found out about his health status.

She began to learn more about HIV and managing the disease. She worked to eliminate stress, which is a leading threat to people living with HIV. The arrival of a grandchild took the attention from her illness and gave her a new focus.

Jackie now shares her experience with others so they can be encouraged and learn how to live with HIV. With women being the leading demographic group contracting the disease, her work has taken on a new urgency. She knows what it's like to hear that diagnosis. She knows what it's like to be 89 pounds and sick. She knows what it's like to have someone tell you your viral load has skyrocketed. All of this, she can share with another sister facing the same struggles. She can help the other woman gain a new perspective and learn how to live again.

Jackie has formed bonds with women others would have turned their backs on. She does this because she knows the importance of this women reaching women movement. She believes, as I do, that each woman we reach is one more who can reach another.

Time and distance can mute the bond women have, but other times, we can pick up right where we left off, even after years apart. Think back to a relationship you've had with another woman who is no longer a regular part of your life. Did you go through a tough time together? Did you share an intense experience? Were you close growing up, in college, or at work? Why are you not close anymore?

As you think over this relationship, you may find now is the perfect time to reconnect. Give her a call. Send her an email. Look her up on Facebook. Reach out to a woman you've not spoken with in a while and renew your friendship.

Whether she is your mother, sister, cousin, old friend, classmate, co-worker, or sorority sister, take the time to make that connection. Today.

WOMEN REACHING WOMEN MOMENT

Consider the women in your workplace, class, neighborhood, apartment building, church, or other setting. Have you formed negative opinions about any of them based on how they speak, dress, or look? Or about what they drive or where they live? All without getting to know them? Is it possible your negative opinion is incorrect? Look for an opportunity to interact with this woman in the coming week and get to know her. It's possible she has a lot more to her than at first glance.

"I can do all this through him who gives me strength." – Philippians 4:13

5 Motherhood Is Our Greatest Role

Jochabed, the mother of Moses, is a good example for motherhood. She was divorced twice. She was forced to make some tough decisions under pressure. There was a decree to kill all the Hebrew boys under two, which meant Jochabed's son Moses would be included in that number. Talk about pressure. How would she save her son?

Motherhood is our greatest ministry and our hardest work. We find joy in the blessing of our children. But we also find frustration in our circumstances, as more and more of us find ourselves doing it all alone. As a result, we are angry that we are faced with the challenges of carrying the entire burden on our own. But God gives us so many joys through our children to replace the anger. The ministry of motherhood itself puts us in a whole other position in life.

Once we become mothers, our focus changes from ourselves to those God has entrusted to our care. Or, at least, that's how it should work. Sometimes we are so compromised that we don't show this maturity. Our interests, desires, and hearts belong to something other than our children. When I was hooked on drugs and on the streets, my children were not my top concern. Drugs had my attention.

When we are out of touch with God, the enemy introduces other things to stand in the way of our relationship with our children. When we finally begin to seek God, we can turn that around.

God blessed me to reclaim the relationship with my children, and today, I am close to each of my three young adults. Rarely a day goes by that my daughter and I do not talk. I consider her one of my dearest friends. And I was honored when she was interviewed for this book and said I was a blessing to her life.

For a parent to have a 22-year-old call them a blessing in this postmodern era is an honor. My daughter said the women reaching women concept has influenced her in a positive way. She doesn't feel the need to follow the crowd or to yield to pressure just to fit in. The strong women she has witnessed over the years have given her a sense of self. I feel joy at this, knowing it means this work is reaching the next generation. My daughter mentors several younger girls through coaching an AAU basketball team. She also founded the Respect Yourself, Check Yourself Protect Yourself (RCP) movement at the University of North Florida during her sophomore year. She uses RCP to teach young girls how to make right choices about sex, drugs, and education.

As for my sons, they speak to me often and we date once a month. I use the dates to catch up on what's going on in their lives, instill values in them, and give them a safe place to share their intimate secrets. I make a point to be wherever my children are. They are on Facebook, so I am on Facebook. They are on Twitter, so I am on Twitter. They like to text message, so I text. I listen to the music they like, watch shows they like. I do all of this because I want to be connected with them. My role as their mother is my most important role of all. Our children basically need affection, which is love; attention, which is time; and acceptance, which is forgiveness.

Sisters, if you have made mistakes where your children are concerned, it's not too late. Our children are resilient. They can take a lot of things we dish out, and by God's grace, they can allow us to make up for some of the poor choices we've made. I feel led by God to share this with you, because I know there is a sister reading this who has made some wrong choices regarding her children and she longs for a sign that those bad choices are not the end of the road.

This is that sign. If I can recover my relationship with my children and develop a close bond with them after the things I put them through when I was hooked on drugs, so can you. That's not to say it will be easy. Repairing the damage done due to poor decisions and neglect can take much effort, much time, and much prayer.

My children were young when I was on drugs. I often left them with family members for weeks on end without so much as a phone call. Sometimes I would be on binges for 21 consecutive days.

But God saw fit to redeem me.

When we reach other women and share our stories as mothers, we can encourage, educate, and enlighten each other. Today I am a single mom with three adult children in three different state universities. They are over eighteen so there is no child support. Being a single parent is difficult. I learn so much from the testimonies of other single moms, especially those who have never been married. Here I am reminded of Paul's letter to Titus. He speaks to Titus about certain groups. He says in Titus 2:3-5: "Likewise, teach the older women to be reverent in the way they live, not to be slanderers or addicted to much wine, but to teach what is good. Then they can urge the younger women to love their husbands and children, to be self-controlled and pure, to be busy at home, to be kind, and to be subject to their husbands, so that no one will malign the word of God."

This is a Biblical mandate for women to reach other women. This isn't just my mission; it's a directive God has given. He so wants us women to reach other women, especially in the area of motherhood.

I believe God calls women to mentor each other because He knows just how difficult motherhood can be. Often, we make decisions, not sure in the moment if they are the right ones. The results of our decisions sometimes aren't known until years and years later when our children are older. To top it off, what worked with one child may not work with another, so we end up confused. When we share our experiences with each other, we can learn different tactics that work and find strategies to fit our situations.

We must make parenting a priority. We have been conditioned by slavery to raise our children in reverse order and we must stop. In slavery the Black woman was conditioned not to trust the Black man to lead, protect, and provide for her. As a matter of fact this, behavior modification theory is outlined in the "Willie Lynch Letter." Please Google and read it. It will change your life forever. The residue of it still impacts us today. It has been passed down through generations. We raise our daughters to be independent, never to need anyone else. We baby our sons and teach them to lean on us. The result is that women are overbearing in relationships because that's the role they saw growing up and it's the only way they know how to be. When we meet men who want to stand up and be the men that God called them to be, conflict arises, because both of us want to be in charge at all times.

When we coddle our sons and refuse to teach them responsibility as they grow up, we do them a disservice. We handicap them when it comes to relationships and make it difficult for them to function as adults. We make decisions for them most of their childhood because we have been conditioned not to trust them to make good choices. .

If a daughter has a situation, we say, "Figure it out, and tell me how you are going to solve your problem." If a son has the same situation, we say, "Here is what you need to do."

So our sons are constantly looking for someone to make decisions for them. We have failed to help them build their intellectual capacity.

Another point I make in here is this: Teach your sons to be responsible young men. Proverbs 31:1-5 depicts a story of King Lemuel's oracle, which his mother taught him. It was his mother who taught him about women, drinking alcohol, and taking care of the needy.

I do the same with my sons. I am teaching them to be men. During our monthly dates, I also teach them how to hold a door, how to treat a woman, how to carry themselves as men. I have frank conversations with them about relationships and life. My sons are 20 and 21. It's a job just policing them and training them how to be gentlemen. It is even a greater job protecting them from cougars (older women) and peer pressure. But I take it as my responsibility because I am their mother.

"Praise be to the God and Father
of our Lord Jesus Christ, who has
blessed us in the heavenly realms
with every spiritual blessing in Christ."
– Ephesians 1:3

6 What You Do Today Changes the Future

I hope by now you've begun to see the urgency for reaching out to other women. We cannot wait. We must be intentional and diligent as we connect. If at first we meet resistance, we must persevere. Not all women will immediately respond to your advances, but this must not deter you. Just keep praying for them and reaching out. Once they see your intentions are pure and your interest sincere, they will warm up to the idea.

What we do from this point forward will determine the type of future we have.

If we each endeavor to reach women in our own way, then the collective effort will create a world like we've never seen before. One woman may choose to reach women by focusing on education. Another may choose to reach women by focusing on economic empowerment. Another may choose to reach women by focusing on health. The needs are so vast and the potential so great that this movement has room for all of this.

But in order to reach out to other women, some of us must first work on a few things ourselves.

Dating and Marital Relationships

Many of us have dreams and ideas and goals of what we feel having a spouse and partner should be. But because of the environment and the state of men in this country, we settle. We hear dire statistics that there is one man for every four women. We look at the newspapers that show male after male being incarcerated. We look around the community and see men who are hooked on drugs and others who are perpetually unemployed. And we see this dismal picture and resolve that it's better to have a piece of man than no man at all. But when we do that, our spiritual woman suffers and battles this reality because she knows we should have better, different, more.

If you fall in love with a man who gets out of prison, has paid his debt to society, is seeking the Lord and working on his hopes and dreams, that's OK. I'm not saying you shouldn't be with him. Everybody makes mistakes and we are all allowed to repent and redeem ourselves.

I'm not talking about that man. The man who is looking to create a better life. No, I'm talking about the man who isn't interested in anything better. The man we talked about when we discussed Abigail. The man who is mean-spirited, foolish, and in no way ready for you.

When we discussed Abigail and the fact that she was married to a man who was foolish, we talked about the fact that we as women must be cognizant of being unequally yoked. When we are unequally yoked and involved in a relationship with a man who does not complement us and does not share our desires or interests in improving life, we automatically set ourselves up for disappointment and conflict. My pastor, the Reverend Marcus Davidson says, "We cannot be tricked by an imitation love."

Sometimes when we initially get with a partner, we do have things in common. But as life changes, we grow. Unfortunately, that partner may not. When that happens, you may find that where you were at first compatible because you were both on the same self-destructive path, you are now incompatible because you have seen the light and are looking to do something different.

I remember when I finally made the choice to get clean and sober for good. As I progressed down the path toward my new life, I realized I could not go back to my first husband. He represented the old life. The life of drugs, alcohol, irresponsible behavior, and strife.

We had at one time been compatible, but now we were not. We didn't want the same things in life. And we did not have the same values. We divorced.

That experience was an important lesson for me. It let me know that I must be with someone who shares my values. There are some times in a relationship where you try working it out. But there are other times when you know you're only prolonging the misery. Divorce is a sin but it is a forgivable sin. God will forgive you.

When you're in a situation where the other person does not want to change for the better or one that endangers your health, happiness, and sanity, it's time to make an exit. And if you are considering a relationship with a person whose values you do not share and whose trajectory in life is downward because of poor choices, don't do it! Don't go there, sister.

I sometimes wonder, using my spiritual imagination, just why Abigail even got with Nabal in the first place? Did she think she could change him? Did he pretend to be someone he was not? I realize in those days arranged marriages were common, so choice may not have been on her side. But what's our excuse? How many times do we end up with men who are simply not good mates for us? We are smart, pretty, outgoing, and educated. Yet, we end up with men who are surly, dumb, and unpleasant. That, or they don't support our dreams.

Let's say you are passionate about starting a catering business but you have a man who says, "Oh, baby, we don't need that. It's too hard. Let's just work right where we are for the rest of our lives. We're comfortable. Let's leave it at that."

That lack of support can slowly stifle you and kill your dream. And what's worse, you will go through life never allowing God's power to flow through you by way of that catering business. In Latin the word sex means six. I believe that a relationship is like a triangle. It has three sides — mind, body, and spirit — for both the male and female. When put together it equals six. The mind is the mental stimulation we get from our partner. He must interest us and keep us going. The body is just a nicer word for sex, which is something God created as a beautiful experience between a man and a wife. The spirit side of that equation refers to that inner part of us, our soul.

Oftentimes we may have two pieces of that equation that match, but we're often missing the third. Usually, that is the spiritual piece. When our partners do not support our hopes and dreams or they try to stand between our connection to the Creator and us, we find the spiritual side of that equation broke. When we are missing the spiritual, we feel hollow inside. We may be going through the motions and look like we are having a good time on the outside, but inside, we are missing something. If your relationship compromises your spiritual life, you are in trouble.

Each of those sides — mind, body, spirit — must be in balance for a healthy you.

Sisters, we truly do not have to settle in our relationships. If you know you are a 10, why settle for a 2? Don't you believe the same God who blessed you to have so many positive attributes is the same God who can bless you with a man who also is full of positive attributes? We don't have to take any man just because he is breathing.

Sometimes we convince ourselves that our relationships are all right. We pretend to be happy, lying even to ourselves. But if you are with someone who does not provide the basic things you require, then you have to ask yourself why you're willing to settle for less than even the basic.

Let's say security and stability are top requirements for me. I want to be with someone who provides those things. In that case, I want someone who has a means of income coming in. That takes care of the financial security. But it may also mean that I need emotional security so I can trust my man. That means I'm not going to have to worry about him sleeping with women in the ministry or anywhere else. It could also mean I need intellectual security. In that case, I need a man who can have an intellectual conversation with me. I want him to open my mind to new ideas. Maybe he's a mechanic so he teaches me about repairing cars. Or maybe he reads up on current events and can talk to me about what's going on in the news.

Stability may mean I need someone who isn't flighty. He's not one thing today and another tomorrow. He is solid, someone I can depend on. I know that if he says something, he means it.

If those are non-negotiable factors for me, then I should not settle for being with someone who does not offer those.

Now, a man may not measure up on every single thing on our sometimes very long lists, but the basics certainly need to be taken care of, if we are to be happy. Whatever you consider basic may be different from what I consider basic, so that's somewhat of a personal choice.

For me, I need my man to show that he loves and respects me. The guy I am dating now literally adores me. It's all over his face. I can show up at a church to preach and three-dozen roses will be waiting for me. If he can't be there in person, he wants to send his presence. I can appreciate that, and it lets me know I am on his mind even when I'm not right in his face.

He grew up seeing his dad adore his mom, so for him, it's nothing new or odd. It's how he is wired.

The Word says don't be unequally yoked. I believe God means that in many ways, including relationship compatibility. You can't be with a man who is so far away from what you are. What will you have in common? What will you talk about? What will hold you together during the tough times? If he is not up to par, don't be seduced into getting with him. Don't think you'll change him after the fact. You won't. But he could change you for the worse.

This is the continuation of the lesson we learned from Abigail's story. Abigail's story highlighted the fact that we must sometimes compensate for a mate's poor choices. The point I make here is that we can avoid mates who habitually make poor choices. We do this by truly studying the character of the person we are considering. Of course, everyone makes a bad decision every now and then. But someone who constantly makes them is not the man for you. His poor judgment will mean he will be a poor provider, will not stand up for you when you need it, and will be the source of much drama.

That goes to a very important point I want you to get when it comes to relationships. If we resolve today to make better choices in men, we will get better results in our relationships. It may mean we must be single a little longer than we want. But that's all right. We can't be spooked by some idea of a "male shortage" or scared that we'll never get a man. If we use the approach I speak of here, we will get a better quality of man. That is because if we study his character before hopping into bed with him or before diving into a relationship, we will know who he is and can avoid (or at least minimize) ugly surprises later on.

***

I was with my last husband for a total of 18 years, including being married for 14. It was a part of my Abigail encounter;

I was married to Nabal for a long time and now I am dating a king. Just as I've said we women do not have to settle in relationships, I also want to remind us that whatever it is we are asking for in a relationship, we must be willing to give.

It's unfair to have a long list of requirements you expect your mate to meet but then you can't measure up. Often, we want the man to add value, but the question becomes: What value are we bringing?

I'm sorry to have to break it down to you, but this book is an honest chat with my sisters. And sometimes, we're asking for more than we can give. Right off, I know that any man I am with will upgrade my life. That's a given. I am not interested in dating anyone who is not bringing something to the table.

But also in that equation is the fact that I will upgrade his life! I will bring something to the table, as well. I can't expect a man to work and put all his money into the bank if I'm not willing to do the same.

Here is another essential point that will save you a lot of grief. Think with your head, not your body. Whether we are 16 or 56, we women sometimes think sex is the thing to get us the man we want. Yet, that's not the case. Sex may get him to connect with us for a few minutes, but it's not the thing to build a strong foundation.

Consider taking the sex out of your unmarried relationship so you can get to know the man in front of you in a different way. This will save you a bit of heartbreak and will allow you to see who is with you because of sex and who is with you because he truly values you.

Health

There is another pressing reason to take the sex out of premarital relationships: HIV and AIDS. HIV, the virus that causes AIDS, is running rampant. And the demographic group that is being diagnosed most often these days is women. Specifically Black women.

When AIDS first came to the public consciousness in the 1980s, people were eager to point to it as a gay disease. It didn't affect them, they were quick to say, if they were heterosexual or in monogamous relationships.

We now know this is absolutely false.

AIDS knows no race, color, creed, age, or gender. It affects everyone. And because it is striking more and more women, we must change our behavior. We no longer have the luxury of casually hopping into bed with a man we do not know and feeling "lucky" if we emerge from there with only our hearts broken. Now, a trip to bed may very well find us HIV positive.

I know quite a bit about this topic. Part of my job as president and CEO of the Mount Olive Development Corporation is to serve families who have been impacted by HIV and AIDS. I have seen families devastating by this disease and the hearts of young girls broken by it.

When we look at protecting ourselves, it starts with being willing to say, "I am worth asking the tough questions." We should be able to discuss our sexual history. We must be willing to get tested together. If he isn't willing to get tested, then we don't need to be together.

As women, we need to understand that if we are sleeping with men and we're not using protection, then we are sleeping with everybody he has slept with or is sleeping with. And in this day of men being on the down-low — sleeping with other men and pretending to be heterosexual — we must be extra vigilant.

But HIV/AIDS is only one health concern we must address. Women often take care of everyone else but forget to take care of themselves. We nurture our men, our parents, our children. The result is that nothing is left for us. So we suffer from stress-related illnesses, poor sleep and nutrition, and declining health due to preventable illnesses we've not paid attention to until too late.

So another change we can make today is to put our health at the top of our priority lists. We must realize that if we are not healthy, then the rest of our family suffers. We can't continue to neglect ourselves. If this sounds like you, sister, promise me — promise yourself — today, that you will make this change. Get the rest you need. If you're depressed or suffering from a prolonged sadness, talk to someone. If you have a nagging health issue, get it checked out. You are too important to God to keep neglecting yourself.

Self-worth

America has painted women into a corner where everything is based on beauty and sex. A lot of times we begin to think our greatest strength or asset is sex. But my mind is my strongest asset. When you say to a man that, "I value myself this much and you're not going to just start sleeping with me because we went out on a few dates," that there is a whole list of requirements, it really gets his attention. It sets you apart. So as Christian women, God has called us and has set us apart. Being priestly means I have to live a certain way and that certain lifestyle might not be common or popular. It may cause me to experience rejection or loneliness but the overall result — when we can think with the end in mind — is a greater level of trust between your mate and you. He knows that you made him wait and you're not going to let anybody just get you in bed. It may sound barbaric or even silly to some, but men need to know they possess their women. And taking sex out of the equation helps them to know that when they do enter into that forever relationship with you and engage in sex, that you truly are theirs.

That automatically sets a different tone for your relationship.

This attitude of being set apart or different is not limited to your dating relationships. Take it into every part of your life. You are special to God. He specifically created you. You are here for a reason and a purpose. When you know this — truly know it — your self-worth immediately increases because you see the value in who you are.

Community Service

In 2002, Dr. Mack King Carter hired me to serve as the president/CEO of the Mount Olive Development Corporation

(MODCO). MODCO is a faith-based, not-for-profit organization incorporated by the New Mount Olive Baptist Church in 1994. MODCO is a faith-based Community Development Corporation whose mission is to revitalize low- and moderate-income communities by providing strategic programs that promote economic development, create jobs, and focus on strengthening families through public services, affordable housing, and entrepreneurial ventures. HIV/AIDS and re-entry are areas of primary interest. In this capacity God has allowed me to serve more than 21,000 low-income families. At MODCO we serve the people nobody else wants to serve — those recovering from addition, incarceration, and dysfunctional family background. Our services include housing and support services for persons who are HIV positive. MODCO has received local, state, and national recognition. We believe that MODCO is our vehicle to take the Gospel from the pulpit to the pavement. It is our way of fulfilling the Isaiah 61 mandate. "The Spirit of the Sovereign Lord is on me, because the Lord has anointed me to proclaim good news to the poor. He has sent me to bind up the brokenhearted, to proclaim freedom for the captives and release from darkness for the prisoners, to proclaim the year of the Lord's favor and the day of vengeance of our God, to comfort all who mourn, and provide for those who grieve in Zion — to bestow on them a crown of beauty instead of ashes, the oil of joy instead of mourning, and a garment of praise instead of a spirit of despair. They will be called oaks of righteousness, a planting of the Lord for the display of his splendor."

All of us at MODCO — I, Jackie, Sharon, and the others — have a story behind the story. We all believe MODCO allows us to serve God by serving others. We are God's instruments of hospitality, hope, and healing in urban poverty stricken communities. Because of our own individual experiences we are convinced that lives can be rebuilt.

Finances

Another change I ask you to make today is in your wallet, sister. Women suffer a lot more when divorce happens than men. Families headed by women are statistically poorer than others. Women earn less than men, on average.

Because of all these reasons, we must begin to pay more attention to our finances. Financial literacy can lead to economic freedom and economic freedom provides options.

We can't leave our finances up to husbands, fathers, men, and brothers. Nor can we bury our head in the sand when it comes to our money.

Develop a practice of living within your means. Do this by creating a budget. And add some giving to the equation. From a spiritual standpoint, God asks us to give 10 percent of our earning to His ministry. So consider setting aside 10 percent of your income for your church or ministry. As we feed into God's work, He feeds into us.

Giving also has another powerful effect. It creates an attitude of wealth. If you find that you regularly give away a certain portion of your income, you will feel more gracious and more abundantly blessed because you will not feel as if every dime you make is consumed with your regular bills.

In addition to giving, set aside something for your own needs. Unexpected — or unplanned — expenses happen. If you have an emergency fund to deal with them, then these things don't have to be a big deal for you. So begin to set aside an emergency fund to cover unexpected or unplanned expenses. If you have no savings at all, your first goal can be to save up $100. This seems like a small amount, but it can have a big effect on you because just knowing you have $100 you've not used gives you a sense of accomplishment.

Your next goal can be to save $1,000. Your ultimate emergency fund goal is to save three to six months of living expenses. That way if you lose your job, get sick, or have a major expense, you have a means to address the issue.

Other money management matters to address are debt and investments. In-depth analysis and advice on these matters are both beyond the scope of this book, but begin to educate yourself about these two issues. Begin to address them. Eliminating debt helps you build wealth because your money is no longer going to interest charges. Investing allows you to create wealth as well by using long-term financial strategies. When you educate yourself about the options in these areas, you find that you will finally be in control of your money. Financial empowerment should be a goal of every woman, because when we are broke and have no money, we cannot minister to our families effectively, provide for our children adequately, or contribute to society in the way we would like.

If the idea of overhauling your finances seems overwhelming, then it is not necessary to do all of these things at once. Do them in stages. For today, just start with one of these ideas — setting up a budget, setting up a savings goal, setting aside a tithe, learning about investments, etc.

WOMEN REACHING WOMEN MOMENT

Look for a volunteer opportunity to help other women in your community. It can be a one-time event or an on-going commitment. Areas of need include — tutorial services, food programs, food drives, women's ministries, etc. Sign up for one of the opportunities.

"For it is by grace you have been saved, through faith – and this is not from yourselves, it is the gift of God."
– Ephesians 2:8

7 Ministries Bring Spiritual Women Ever Closer

My ministry to women began as a Bible study. I thought if I could bring women together and teach them through the lives of women of the Bible, then we could really have something powerful in the name of God. As we began to connect with women in that Bible study, the Holy Spirit began to deal with me about women needing a time to come together. I was studying the story of Esther. I paid attention to when Esther was ready to change things, the first thing she did was call the handmaidens. She had a support group of women — women reaching women. Then they called the whole nation into fasting and praying. That grabbed me. I needed to bring women together to pray.

The community women's Bible study grew into so many other elements of my ministry. Women Reaching Women, which I founded in 2004 at Mount Olive Baptist Church in Fort Lauderdale, Florida, has served more than 1,500 women across the country. It is designed to captivate the very heart of women so they feel the very obvious presence of God in their lives through Bible study, prayer, and other spiritual disciplines.

We started with a small group of about 20 women studying Rick Warren's Purpose Driven Life. The Reverend Lori Morton, Minister Michelle Rolle, and I served as the small group facilitators. This study helped many of the women move from a place of feeling useless to feeling specially created by God. Once we wrapped up the eight-week small group study, we held a series of life skills workshops to enhance women's knowledge of key coping and success skills and strategies. We then held our first Women of Destiny Conference. Our church had held successful women's conferences before, but this one was designed to minister to the whole woman — mind, body, and spirit. It offers a self-awareness program for women. It is comprised of a general workshop series that focuses on spiritual enrichment and includes topics like faith, prayer, and intimacy with God. It includes a special interest workshop series that focuses on topics like marriage, singleness, aging, and grief. It also provides strategies to stop the spread of HIV/AIDS to include free HIV testing and counseling, cancer awareness information, and a forum for discussing domestic violence, depression, and suicide. This conference has attracted women from across the country who represent more than 21 different churches and four denominations.

In October of 2005 I was diagnosed with Hodgkin's Lymphoma in my throat. It would become a two-year fight for my life. During this time my husband of 18 years divorced me and my grandmother who raised me died. My life was turned upside down. The pain was overwhelming. This winter season in my life took my ministry to women to another level. There were sisters like Shelia Pettis and Gwen Elliott who drove me to chemotherapy. Sisters like Doris Love and Patricia Hunter who cooked for me. And sisters like Margaret, Claudia, and Lelia who got their husbands to cook dinner for me and my kids four times a week. There were many brothers who helped me as well but this discussion is focused on women. Women came together and helped minister to me as God restored my body and spirit. This experience gave a new meaning to women reaching women. I became ever more aware of the potential, power, and pressing need for an active network of women working together to touch the lives of other women. I started having an annual holiday prayer breakfast to bring women together to network in December leading up to Kwanzaa.

On November 7, 2009 Dr. Rosalind Osgood Ministries International hosted its first Morning Glory Event. We started traveling around the world bringing together 1000 women in white in prayer. We call it Morning Glory. The white is symbolic of the Glory of God. We structure the program to include all women. The program has a multicultural, multigenerational, and multidenominational flavor to it.

I will never forget the day it began. We assembled at the Mount Zion A.M.E. Church in Oakland Park, Florida. The Reverend Dallasteen Yates, senior pastor, graciously hosted us. We had more than 700 women present. We had 55 churches represented. The women were ages 5 to 89. We also had three faithful husbands to attend: Bishop Gerald Green, Elder Roger Grimes, and the Reverend Raton Remikie. These husbands continue to support our efforts.

This was an awesome encounter with God. It was an overwhelming experience as God poured out His Spirit through his handmaids. Our prayer focus was women. We started with two selections from Minister Genie Rumph and the Women of the St. Johns Missionary Baptist Church in Boyton Beach, Florida. The Reverend Lance Chaney, Senior Pastor of St. Johns Missionary Baptist Church in Boyton Beach, Florida, chartered two buses and sent 80 women from his church, which was more than 50 miles away. Sister Janice Hayes, a renowned orator and community activist, was our mistress of ceremony. Praise and worship was led by Pastor Yates in English followed by two sisters from Iglesia Cristina "Promesas de Vidal" in Spanish. Then the Model prayer was prayed in English, Spanish, and Creole. The individual prayer warriors included: Judge Ilona Holmes, Broward Circuit Court judge, Evangelist Gloria Jackson Richardson of New Shiloh Missionary Baptist Church in Miami, and Pastor Toni Charles from Shiloh Missionary Baptist Church in Daytona Beach. Other program participants included Minister Kimberly Wade, the Reverend Joyce Wright, First Lady Aurilla Grimes, Co-Pastor Connie Morton, Minister Latilda Jahorie, Pastor Novlet Green, and Sister Sharetta Remikie.

I realize I gave a lot of details about that first Morning Glory celebration, but I did so to show you the support we had, even from the outset. When God gives you a women-reaching-women mission, He will give you a means to carry it out in an amazing way.

Out of Morning Glory the Women Reaching Women Word Network was birthed. It is a morning conference call connecting women all over the country. The Women Reaching Women Word Network presents a daily forum each Monday through Friday for women to connect for proclamation, prayer, and praise at 6:30 a.m. Eastern Standard Time.

Our calls are filled with sermons, testimonies, prayers, and praise. This is a powerful way to begin the day. It allows me to connect my sisters from across the country. It also provides a platform for female clergy. We average more than 200 callers per morning.

The year 2010 was very fruitful for the ministry. We gave birth to our leadership institute in Fort Lauderdale, Florida. We invited 12 women to go through our leadership curriculum that includes sessions on prayer, unity, spiritual gifts, team ministry, and leadership. Each woman was also challenged to give birth to a ministry.

***

As result of the challenge, we now have a mentoring ministry for high school girls called Princess in Pink, created by Sister Sharetta with my daughter Shennette being the lead Princess. Princess in Pink is a ministry that allows college-aged women to mentor high school girls. This does several things. One, it creates a bond between the older girls and the younger ones. Two, it teaches the young women to be responsible and provides a vehicle where they can take on a leadership role.

This ministry also gives the younger girls a safe place to share their hopes, goals, dreams, and questions. They get spiritually based answers to their most pressing questions about things going on in their lives.

We also have SPICES, which was created by sister Cecelia Vickers. SPICES is our outreach to single moms. We meet monthly with single moms under 25.

We also have Family Connections, which was created by Sister Annette. Family Connections allows us to provide support to low-income families through mentorship, educational workshops, and peer-to-peer relationships for the purpose of promoting prenatal care and healthy infants. In January 2011 we added four other leadership teams with sisters in Boyton Beach and Daytona Beach, Florida, as well as Philadelphia, Pennsylvania, New York, and Kansas. Each team will meet monthly face-to-face or via conference call. God will use technology to make the leadership institute global. We will eventually have leadership teams across the world.

Within Dr. Rosalind Osgood Ministries (DROM), I have identified 12 women to take on different aspects of the ministry. These women, my daughters in the ministry, get the opportunity to utilize their gifts. I find that allowing them to perform certain tasks helps build their confidence, spiritual knowledge, and ability to witness.

I'm a midwife. My job is to help other women give birth to ministries and purpose. When I help a woman become stronger in ministry, that helps me fulfill the thing God has called us all to do, and that is to spread His Word to the ends of the earth.

I have this one woman, a Jamaican native, by the name of Evangelist Michelle Richards Phillips, who faithfully attends all our DROM activities. I noticed she was on every call and participated in every event. That told me she was serious. She was committed to everything we were doing. When she was laid off from her job, I invited her to be a co-host on a new conference call. This one is at midday and is focused on prayer. This gave her a sense of accomplishment and responsibility. She was able to step out of the crowd and take on a different role within the ministry. Evangelist Phillips has her own ministry, Visions International Ministries, that is designed to identify and promote Gospel artists.

Having her to co-host that prayer call has really connected my Jamaican sisters to the ministry. And to me, that is what this work is all about — it is multicultural and multigenerational. I am in a movement to share Jesus Christ with women all over the world. The conference call is just one of many I want to add.

I want as many conference calls as we can have. Maybe there will be one for pastors. Maybe there will be one for CEOs. Maybe there will be one for strippers. The point is to reach people where they are. Evangelist Phillips and I will bring our ministries together for the first time in 2011 as we sponsor our first annual "Feeding the Hungry Souls" crusade to Jamaica. We are praying that this crusade will serve as a best practices paradigm for women to collaborate and come together for ministry efforts.

My work has recently expanded to include a men's morning conference call as well. Our work is never about excluding men in an extreme way. While we focus on women, men are welcome to be a part of our work. In fact, we have some strong couples in the ministry. Women's ministry must teach women to honor, respect, and reverence our men. Some of the men have gained a whole new perspective by listening in on our calls and hearing from women about their real hurts and hopes. By the way, one of the faithful husbands, Elder Roger

Grimes, senior pastor of the Fort Lauderdale Church of God in Christ, started the Men Connecting Men Everywhere Word Network for men three months after he secretly listened in on the women's call. The men's call attracts men from across the country. I am very proud of this group of men. They are men who love the Lord. They love their wives. They are modeling priestly attributes as they lead in various communities, churches, and homes.

The men invite me to speak on the men's call occasionally. Of course when I am on the men's call, I always share things men need to know about women. I call these Lessons from the Beauty Salon. So I speak to the men on behalf of women everywhere, on behalf of their wives. I do so because we women come to men with so much baggage. Sometimes it's hard for us to talk to them directly and it's hard for them to understand our needs. When I am able to speak on behalf of women in a way that informs men and helps them consider things they've never thought about before, then that is still a women's ministry, even though it is on a men's prayer call. No matter where I go or what capacity I am operating in, my aim is always to do something to touch the lives of women.

The men's and women's calls do various street outreach projects together. Thanksgiving Day 2010, our evangelism coordinator, the Reverend Raton Remikie, organized an outreach initiative in which both calls came together to feed and witness to the homeless. We distributed more than 200 meals, 101 tracts, and prayed with more than 50 individuals. Men have a strong presence in this ministry. They are a part of our prophetic intercessory prayer team that prays for people immediately following the 6:30 am call and a part of the People to People Midday intercessory team.

November 2010 we hosted our first 500 Men in Denim in Prayer. We assembled the men to pray for the women. Men were standing in the gap for women. Elder Ron Harper, associate minister at the Fort Lauderdale Church of God in Christ, was our master of ceremony. These mighty men of God prayed for their mothers, wives, daughters, aunties, and baby mamas. It was an awesome encounter. Pastor Jerri Butler says that this event ministered to her. She says, "To see these men actually praying for women really blessed me."

WOMEN REACHING WOMEN MOMENT

Look for a ministry at church or in your community that focuses on women. Consider how your skills, talents, and gifts can be a help to this ministry. Offer your services.

"This righteousness is given through faith in Jesus Christ to all who believe." – Romans 3:22

8 What Will You Do Now, Sister?

I have laid out my case for a multicultural, multigenerational, multidenominational movement for women to reach other women. You know this is a historic call that can have a far-reaching impact. You now realize so many of our challenges stem from not liking, knowing, or trusting each other. And you also know that we are the solution to so many ills. If we act on what we know, we can change not just our lives for the better, but the lives of our children, families, communities, and indeed, the world!

This concept can bring us out of LoDebar, that barren place of nothingness. Once this idea of women reaching women catches on and grows, a network of sisters all over the world will help to ensure that no sister lingers in that place.

So what will you do with this knowledge? Will you begin today to reach out to other women? Will you join me in this cause?

Making any change can be intimidating or scary. If you've not been one to form relationships with other women, then the call to intentionally reach out to them may cause you to run the other way. But as with any positive change, the results produced can make any momentary discomfort well worth it. Just give sisterhood a try. If you're nervous about doing it on your own, enlist a friend, cousin, sister, or other woman to team up with you.

If you want to start by reaching out on an individual basis, that is wonderful. Follow some of the suggestions I've given in this book. Reach out to a sister you see who is in need.

If you want to join me in my work with Women Reaching Women, I welcome you. We have many opportunities where your service will be welcome and needed.

We are expanding the conference calls, we are holding events in cities across the world, and we are adding new ministries. If you have a heart to serve, we have a place for you. Join this mega movement.

Hit me on Facebook at Rosalind Osgood or e-mail me at drosgood@yahoo.com. You can learn more at my Website, www.droministries.com.

Women reaching women is a movement that must grow. I cannot do it alone. God has called each of us to be a part of

touching lives. There is a story behind your story.
Let's connect.

WOMEN REACHING WOMEN MOMENT

Invite your girlfriends out to lunch or dinner to discuss this book and ways you each can reach other women. Be specific. And then act upon the ideas that come out of the discussion.

"Do not judge, or you too will be judged." – Matthew 7:1

About the Author

Dr. Rosalind Osgood is a former welfare mom who lived on the streets of Fort Lauderdale, Florida. Faith in God and the help of numerous men and women enabled her to change her life in a profound way. Today, she is sober and free of the drugs and alcohol that sent her to homelessness. She also has build strong relationships with her three children, who are attending three different state universities.

She earned both her Master's and Doctoral degrees in Public Administration from Nova Southeastern University. In December 2007, she earned a Master's of Divinity Degree from New Orleans Southern Baptist Theological Seminary. The Rev. Osgood has the unique distinction of being the first woman in the history of the New Mount Olive Baptist Church to be licensed, ordained, and positioned in the pulpit by the world renowned Dr. Mack King Carter, pastor emeritus of the New Mount Olive Baptist Church of Fort Lauderdale, Florida.

She is the president and CEO of Mount Olive Development Corporation, where she has seen new programs created to reach those recovering from addiction, homelessness, and incarceration. She also is an adjunct professor at Nova Southeastern University, where she teaches ethics, strategic management, leadership, public policy, and other subjects. She also is a consultant who helps organizations in the areas of strategic planning, organizational development, and leadership.

Dr. Osgood is the founder of Women Reaching Women women's ministry. She has received many awards for her leadership and humanitarian efforts.

To learn more about her ministry, including the Women Reaching Women Word Network, visit www.drministries.com.

Write to her at drosgood@yahoo.com.

Get Involved!

Join the Women Reaching Women World Network Monday through Friday at 6:30 a.m. Eastern Standard Time for prayer, inspiration, and encouragement. Call (605) 475-4860, then enter code 929107#.

To inquire about booking Dr. Osgood to speak at your conference, retreat, convention, or other event, e-mail her at drosgood@yahoo.com. Please include your event's purpose, date, and requested discussion topic.